D1595106

Take it to the Limit

The Dave Mungenast Way

By Ed Youngblood

Published by Motohistory
for Dave Mungenast
Classic Motorcycles LLC,
St. Louis, Missouri

All photos have been provided by members of the Mungenast family or their friends and associates. Every effort has been made to credit photographers when that information was available.

Cover design by Kim Barlag.
Main dust cover photo by Dick Lague.

Books are available in single copies or quantity from
Dave Mungenast Classic Motorcycles LLC
5625 Gravois Road
St. Louis, MO 63116
Phone: 314-481-1291
Fax: 314-481-2629
E-mail: classicmotorcycles@davemungenast.com
Web Site: http://www.classicmotorcyclesllc.com

ISBN 0-9788817-0-2

5 4 3 2 1

Printed in the United States

Contents

Foreword

It is 4:30 a.m. somewhere in the pine trees near the starting line of the 84th Annual Pikes Peak Hill Climb. I am sipping coffee in my pickup while crews are busy unloading and preparing their race cars for qualifying. I am asking myself—why am I here? At age 69, I don't need this. My alarm went off at 3:20 a.m. But there is a need: I have two sons—Wally, Jr. and Paul Dallenbach—racing against each other in the same class of open wheel racers.

I begin to quietly reminisce about some of the great times on this mountain, one of which was the 9th Annual Colorado 500 in 1984. A close friend of mine, Nick Sanborne, President of the Pikes Peak Hill Climb, arranged for our entire group to ride, or race, your preference, to the top of the mountain. Pikes Peak was ours for one hour, and our group photo was priceless. Everyone was smiling. It included Dan Gurney, Pancho Carter, Jerry Grant, and yes, Dave Mungenast, to name just a few of 180 riders. The experience and the relationships that grew from it were special, like mine with Dave. Back through the years Dave, Al Unser, and I had the opportunity to ride together, and it didn't take long for us to realize that Dave had a lot more talent and experience than we did on two wheels.

I didn't know a whole lot about Dave then; only that we were about the same age, raising some kids, and making a living with anything that burned gasoline or methanol. As the years went by,

Colorado 500 riders at Pikes Peak summit, 1984.

our friendship became stronger as we realized we had so much in common. We grew up in our era of icons such as Marlon Brando, Elvis Presley, Marilyn Monroe, James Dean and other heroes of the '50s and '60s. We have been blessed with many opportunities and fortunate enough to live exciting and fulfilling lives. 2006 will be Dave's 25th time to participate in the Colorado 500.

There are many stories in this well-prepared book about Dave Mungenast and his family, his friends, and our family of the Colorado 500. All of us are proud to know Dave, Barbara, Dave Jr., Ray, Kurt, and what they have accomplished in life.

As I think of Dave, I recall the 30th Annual Colorado 500 in 2005. Dave was so busy with other commitments that he couldn't make registration day or the start of the event. So his secretary, Patty Ramsey, and his boys, Ray, Kurt and Dave, Jr., collectively made arrangements to fly Dave into the Gunnison airport around noon on Monday, the first day the route took us through Gunnison, where we all come for fuel and lunch. I was there to pick Dave up at the airport, and I remembered that he looked tired and drawn, and knew it had been a long week for him, with many responsibilities, and that it was hard for him to get there. I said to myself, "This is a testimony to what Dave is all about." He wanted to be there for his friends and his sons. His motorcycle and riding gear were waiting for him at a motorcycle dealership in town, and I noted that by the time Dave suited up and mounted his iron horse, the sparkle in his eyes had returned.

We are proud to know Dave, his family, and his many friends. This book captures the man, his goals, his faith, and his generosity for us to admire for years to come. Dave, we are proud to be your friends.

Wally Dallenbach

Introduction and Acknowledgment

I first met Dave Mungenast at the Isle of Man in 1971. I had been on the staff of the American Motorcyclist Association for just a year at that time, and he was riding his fifth International Six Days Trial, on his way to winning his third gold medal. Over the next three decades we would see each other frequently at motorcycle industry functions, though we were often going in different directions, like passing ships plying the same sea. He was a friendly, smiling, and courteous man, sometimes wearing a loud shirt.

After 28 years of service, I left the AMA in 1999, seeking the opportunity to focus on the things I enjoyed most about motorcycling, which usually centered on history and heritage, including vintage and classic motorcycles. By this time, Dave Mungenast had built a very successful career in automobile and motorcycle sales, and commercial development. His sons were running the established businesses, and Dave had turned his attention toward new business development and philanthropic interests. This is where our two ships began to move toward the same shipping lanes. Dave opened his own motorcycle museum in St. Louis the following year, by which time we had both been inducted into the Motorcycle Hall of Fame. I was doing curatorial work for several museums, including the Guggenheim Art of the Motorcycle Exhibition, and it was my business to work with leading motorcycle collectors throughout the nation, including Dave. For this reason, and due to the fact that we were both beginning to attend many of the nostalgic gatherings of motorcycle industry "old timers," Dave and I found an opportunity to know each other better than we had over the previous thirty years.

In 2004, I spoke with the Mungenast sons, Dave, Jr., Ray, and Kurt, about the idea of writing a biography on Dave. I had previously written biographies on John Penton and Dick Mann, who are motorcyclists of high achievement and fascinating character. I could count in single digits the men I have known in the motorcycle industry to whom I was willing to devote the time and energy required for a biography, and Dave Mungenast is one of them.

I have many people to thank for their assistance and support of this project, certainly the greatest of which are the Mungenast family: Dave, Barbara, and their three sons. This has not been an easy project for Dave. Dave loves other people, he loves gatherings, and he loves adventure and excitement, but he prefers never to be the center of attention. His natural humility conflicted with the whole idea, yet he readily gave me time from his busy schedule for nearly a dozen interviews, and even a three-day tour of his rural properties in Missouri. At one point I mistook his cooperation for comfort with the process, and I asked, "Are you becoming comfortable with what we are doing?" He said, "No, you have to understand that this is extremely awkward for me." Yet he continued to suppress his own feelings and respond readily to my every request. I found Barbara of a similar humble nature. She spoke to me excitedly and at length about her sons, but was reticent to talk about herself. Rather, she wanted Dave to remain that center of attention he didn't want to be.

I want to thank Dave, Jr., Ray, Kurt, and Dave Larsen for being my reality checkers. They have read the manuscript while it was in progress, and caught my misunderstandings and historical errors. Especially, I want to thank Dave Larsen, who was named official project coordinator. He helped me with research, finding phone numbers, and scheduling interviews. Patty Ramsey generously helped in a similar fashion, providing information and arranging the opportunities when I could wedge my way into Dave's incredible schedule. Tina Yeager and Vatia Flach helped guide me through the complexity of ManCo. And thanks also to Don Levin for helping me better understand the retail car business. Carl and Virginia Mungenast helped with family history, and Carl especially gave me fine insights into the dynamics of the Mungenast family.

Approximately a hundred interviews were conducted for this book, many of which were with Mungenast employees. I say to them, I know how uncomfortable it must have been to have some guy coming around asking all kinds of questions about your boss. If you read this, I hope you will take comfort in the fact that no confidences have been betrayed and no one has been defamed. At least, I hope not.

When I began this project, I suspect I suffered from many of the common assumptions about the retail automobile business: that it is deceptive, cut-throat, and mean. I knew Dave as a genuinely thoughtful, compassionate, and considerate person, and I expected it would be interesting to learn how the man might be reconciled with his livelihood. I wondered if I might find a hard person hiding beneath the veneer, but this was not the case. Honesty and extraordinary deference to others are not just a façade through which Dave does business. Rather, they are the keystones of his business organization. They exist at the core of the Dave Mungenast Way, and he has woven them—with the support of hundreds of loyal and like-minded employees—into the very fabric of his success. I only hope that this story accurately conveys both the man and his methodology, and the reasons the two are consistent and inseparable.

Ed Youngblood

CHAPTER ONE

The Mungenasts of St. Louis

In 1847, Reinhardt Mungenast and his 12-year-old son Benedict, born in 1835 in the German state of Baden, immigrated to America and settled in St. Louis. Benedict became a citizen in 1858, and three years later joined the Missouri Infantry as a private to fight on the side of the North in the American Civil War. His father also joined the ranks, enlisting in the Illinois Cavalry in January, 1863. Both in Europe and America, the mid-19th century was a period of social upheaval and political revolution. Ideas of liberty, equality, and fraternity had spread outward from the French Revolution, throughout Europe. Industrialization, migration to the cities and mill towns, and population growth had uprooted society, and discontent became focused on the monarchies and aristocracy-based governments that were in control of the old order. In 1848, all of Europe erupted in political revolution. Widespread demand for representation and relief from oppression resulted in the rise of parliaments and the weakening of the aristocracy.

Among the leading powers of Europe, only Germany remained fragmented and decentralized, comprised of small states run by petty rulers, bargaining their allegiance between Prussia to the north and Austria to the south. The lack of progress toward reform within the Germanic states resulted in a wave of immigration, mostly to North America. Many of these emigrants were from an educated class, seeking greater political, economic, and religious freedom. Those arriving in the United States quickly moved west, pursuing dreams of opportunity. Cities like Milwaukee, Cincinnati, Columbus, and St. Louis developed large centers of German culture, and German became a second language. St. Louis and its surroundings were aggressively promoted as a desirable place for German emigrants by Gottfried Duden, a civil official from Cologne who came to America, settled near St. Charles, and undertook a one-man letter writing campaign in praise of the climate, fertility, resources, freedom, and opportunities of the Missouri River valley, likening it to the Rhineland.[1] German emigrants set up businesses, banks, militias, newspapers, and cultural institutions, such as theater and opera companies. Many were Catholic, and religion became a strong unifying influence in their emerging communities. Like the Mungenast men, great numbers enlisted to fight in the War Between the States, which seemed a natural extension of the pursuit of freedom that had caused them to leave Europe. Historian William Faherty writes, "Self-reliant, they abhorred the institution of slavery. Their activities on the south side [of St. Louis] . . . centered around gymnastic societies, singing clubs, song circles, and the beer gardens. Gymnastic societies were to play their part in toning up the muscles of many a volunteer for the Union forces."[2]

St. Louis held a special place in America's epic civil war. One year before the arrival of Reinhardt and Benedict Mungenast, the slaves Dred and Harriett Scott filed suit in St. Louis Circuit Court in pursuit of their freedom. More than a decade later, their claim was denied by the United States Supreme Court, a rancorous decision that contributed significantly to the tension between free and slave states that led to the outbreak of war. We do not know how these developments affected the young Benedict Mungenast, but watching one of the major dramas in the buildup to war take place in his adopted city during his teenage years may

[1] The influence of German emigrants on the growth, culture, and economy of St. Louis is discussed in greater detail by Father William Barnaby Faherty, S.J. in "St. Louis: A Concise History," published by the St. Stanislaus Historical Museum Society, 2004.

[2] William Barnaby Faherty, S.J. "St Louis: A Concise History," page 48.

well have influenced his decision to enlist, even before his father. In fact, St, Louis, sitting both geographically and ideologically on the cusp between North and South, remained a special place throughout the Civil War. The high concentration of Germans and their well-trained militias was a factor in swinging the city toward the side of the North, but many native residents remained in sympathy with the South, leading to civil disorder that caused St. Louis to be held under marshal law for the duration of the war.

Reinhardt Mungenast, the patriarch of the American Mungenasts, traced his lineage to the mid-17th century and the village of Mathon in the Austrian province of Tyrol. According to Emmerich Mungenast, still living in Austria, *Muthana*, or "mountain," can be found in the name of a farm in the region called *Muthana aste.* From this we derive the modern name "Mungenast," which can mean "mountain farm." The use of the words in a surname in the 17th century and earlier would have literally meant ". . . from the mountain farm," or perhaps just ". . . from the mountain."[3]

Records from as late as the 18th century show the name spelled "Munggenast" and sometimes "Munkenast." With branches of the family that immigrated to Luxembourg and German Alsace, the name has appeared variously as "Monkenast" and "Moshernast," the latter perhaps reflecting a French pronunciation. One derivation found on a record in America—perhaps recorded phonetically in error—says "Monkenhorst." With the advancement of the printed word and the standardization of language, "Mungenast" has emerged as the standardized modern spelling of the name.

The family was not wealthy or from the upper strata of Austrian society, but earned significant prominence through the achievements of Joseph Munggenast, born in Schnann in 1680. As an architect and master builder under the tutelage of his uncle Grand Masterbuilder Jacob Prandtauer, Joseph earned recognition as the designer and builder of many churches, monasteries, and government buildings in the Baroque style. In that era, such construction was seen not just as a building project executed

[3] For early Mungenast genealogy and history we are indebted to David Mungenast, son of Carl, nephew of Dave Mungenast, Sr., and great-great grandson of Benedict Mungenast, who compiled a family history in preparation for a Mungenast family reunion that took place in August, 2000.

anonymously by a construction crew, but as a personal and singular work of art. The masterbuilder served not only as the architect, but selected materials and supervised construction. He had to be accomplished in design, engineering, and stonemasonry, and often had many projects in progress. Major projects could consume a significant period of his career, and some would extend beyond his lifetime and be taken up by his son or protégé. Joseph Munggenast is credited with scores of major religious and secular buildings, some of which are considered masterpieces of the Baroque style. As an engineer and stonemason, he also consulted on major road projects.

The late 17th century was a period of great capital investment and reconstruction in Lower Austria. The Turkish invasion had been turned back after laying waste to the region, and both the Catholic Church and the nobility were eager to reassert themselves through the construction of great and impressive buildings. This provided Joseph Mungenast a fertile and lucrative working environment. As the prominent masterbuilder of the region, Joseph is credited as founder of the Lower Austrian Line of the family. Other nations of Europe were equally in need of such skills, and his younger brother Sigismund, born in 1694, moved to Northern Europe where he became head of the Luxembourg Line of the family. Another branch of the family immigrated to the German state of Baden. The earliest patriarch of this line on record was Johannes Munggenast, born in Fehrbach in 1688. It is from this line that Benedict and the Mungenasts of St. Louis descended.[4]

Benedict Mungenast married Louisa Wunch in January 1856. This union produced two sons, Andrew and Joseph. In 1894, the brothers went into business together, founding the Model Hardware Company, located at 3215 Meramac Street in the area of St. Louis known as South City. In addition to a wide range of tools and supplies, the company offered repair for stoves, ranges, washing machines, and lawn mowers. An article published in a neighborhood newspaper circa 1924 spoke of their

[4] Though we leave the Mungenasts of Europe at this stage of our story, the family has continued to produce individuals of note. For example, Mathias Mungenast served as Finance Minister of Luxembourg from 1882 to 1916, and briefly as Prime Minister. Furthermore, Ernst-Moritz Mungenast (1898–1956) was a very popular novelist in Germany who enjoyed sales of more than a million copies of his various titles during his lifetime, and remains highly-regarded as a leading literary talent of his era.

fairness and integrity. It read, "Their goods are all marked in plain figures, and when the lady of the house is busy attending to her duties, she can safely send her little child to do the buying for her, for there it will receive the same attention and the same price as if she herself would go." The article continues, "This shows that the Mungenast Brothers conduct their business in a straightforward, conscientious manner, and this is undoubtedly the cause of the success they have obtained."[5]

Andrew, the elder brother, born in 1864, married Elizabeth Spindler in May, 1884, and produced six children: These included Andrew G., born in 1895; Francis Louisa, born in 1896, and four other siblings—Andrew Joseph, Elizabeth, Maria Theresa, and Katherina—who died in infancy between 1885 and 1896. The oldest living son, Andrew G., married Charlotte Boekel, daughter of a yeast manager at the Anheuser Busch brewery. This union resulted in six children: Andrew, Thomas, Charlotte P., John, David, and Carl. There were five years between John and David, and another six before Carl arrived. The reason was that Charlotte was declared dead during the birth of John, due to heart failure. She was revived, but it was some time before she could again risk bearing children. While many of the siblings will figure in our story of *The Dave Mungenast Way*, our focus will be on David, christened David Francis Mungenast and known within the family today as Dave, Sr.

Andrew and Charlotte built their marriage on traditional German Catholic values. Andy, as his friends called him, was the provider and disciplinarian; Charlotte was the nurturer and homemaker. Charlotte, who had converted to Catholicism from the Episcopalian Church, was better educated than her husband. Their youngest son, Carl, reports, "Mom was a very smart lady before it was fashionable for women to be bright. She had a lot of organizational ability. Both parents were high achievers." He adds, "She was also known within the family as 'the velvet sledgehammer.' She was persuasive and persistent, and rarely failed to get her way. We kids could disagree with her about how to do something. Two days latter we were doing it her way and wondering, 'How did that happen?'"

Andy was an idealist and a deeply religious man who exhibited a strong work ethic and sense of responsibility toward his community. Dave Mungenast recalls, "My father worked six

[5] Page 62, undated issue of "South Saint Louis," Missouri Historical Society.

Andrew and Charlotte Mungenast, early 1970s

days a week and went to mass every day." Younger brother Carl concurs: "Father had a deep and abiding faith. He believed that there is a God and a hereafter, and that we are rewarded for our works." Oldest son Andrew, Jr. states, "He was a generous and charitable man who would give away his last dollar if he thought someone else needed it." Carl agrees, "Our father was generous to a fault. He genuinely believed that God would provide for our needs. Our mother, who was more practical and concerned about the welfare of the family, sometimes strongly objected to his charity." By way of example, Carl relates, "One time we were discussing some need of the family at the dinner table. Dad said, 'God will provide,' and Mom responded, 'Well, he better get down here soon because the refrigerator is going out!'" Yet, Andy's firm belief in divine reward for good works was the foundation for an honesty, integrity, and dedication to community that have remained evident in his children. Carl explains, "We were taught accountability by our parents. What's right is right and you get out of life what you put into it."

Andy Mungenast, a World War One Navy veteran with an eighth-grade education, earned his living as director of sales and advertising for Streckfus Steamers, a company that managed excursion boats on the Mississippi River. Streckfus owned the Admiral, based in St. Louis, and the President, docked in New Orleans. At one time or another, all but Carl among the Mungenast children had jobs aboard the Admiral. The boat is still a feature on the local waterfront, now permanently fixed on pilings in the Mississippi. Perhaps this exposure to the great and restless Mississippi may have helped imbue young David with his sense of adventure, just as it had with a boy named Sam Clemens, raised a century earlier just upriver in Hannibal.

Bill Streckfus, who knew Andy from an early age, then grew up to become Captain of the Admiral in 1963, recalls, "It was a pleasure to work with him. He was one of the few people you will ever meet in your life that you've never heard anyone say something bad about. He was talkative, friendly, one of the best public speakers I have ever heard, and seemed to know everyone in St. Louis, including business leaders, local politicians, and Senators and Congressmen." When the Jefferson Memorial Expansion Monument was being planned along the river front during the 1950s, Streckfus and other businesses along the river objected to an early design that would entirely cut off access to the river. Andy Mungenast became instrumental in negotiating with the U.S. Parks Service to modify the plan to provide better access to the landings. Captain Streckfus asserts, "We could never have accomplished it without Andy. He had access to all the right people in St. Louis and Washington to put forward and get approval of a modified plan that benefited the businesses that used the river."

But it was not his day job with Streckfus where Andy Mungenast made his permanent mark. On October 13, 1915, at the Mission Inn on South Grand Avenue in St. Louis, he, along with Henry Giessenbier, Jr. became a co-founder of the Junior Chamber of Commerce, known today as the Jaycees. Originally, the organization was named the Young Men's Progressive Civic

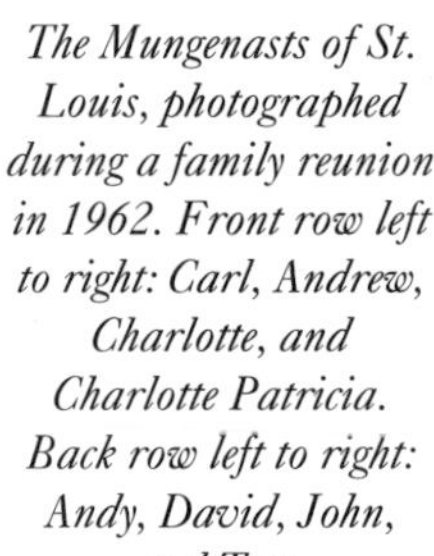

The Mungenasts of St. Louis, photographed during a family reunion in 1962. Front row left to right: Carl, Andrew, Charlotte, and Charlotte Patricia. Back row left to right: Andy, David, John, and Tom.

Association. Giessenbier was its first president and Andy Mungenast its first secretary. Because the organization focuses on the promotion of civic responsibility in young businessmen, the official "retirement age" in the Jaycees is 36, but Andy Mungenast remained active until his death at age 80, empowered to continue his service to the organization under the title of "Honorary President." In his book entitled *The First 25 Years of the Junior Chamber of Commerce*, historian John Armbruster of St. Louis wrote, "Perhaps the one man who stands out for continuous loyalty to the idea and who did perhaps more than any other to carry on the hard work of keeping the struggling organization together was Andrew G. Mungenast. When he joined Henry Giessenbier in the Jaycee movement, he was in it for life."[6]

In an interview on the occasion of the Jaycees' 50th anniversary, Andy Mungenast said, "I owe everything I've got to the Junior Chamber of Commerce. I'm just an ordinary guy who only finished grade school, but thanks to the organization I got the rough spots smoothed down."[7] Mungenast went on to explain, "I

[6] Page 28, "St Louis Commerce," October 1976

[7] "St. Louis Post-Dispatch," October 14, 1965.

The Mungenast family reunion in 1962. Dave is in the top row on the far right. Barbara, with infant David Jr. on her lap is in the second row, second from left.

was so bashful it wasn't even funny. It was after I got into the Jaycees that I got where I could stand up in front of people and talk." It is characteristic of his philosophy of service that Andy Mungenast volunteered countless hours over most of his lifetime to the organization, yet he saw himself as the beneficiary. Through the Jaycees, he was a tireless booster of his community.

Dave's father, Andy Mungenast, on the Mississippi River with the excursion boat Admiral in the background, late 1960s.

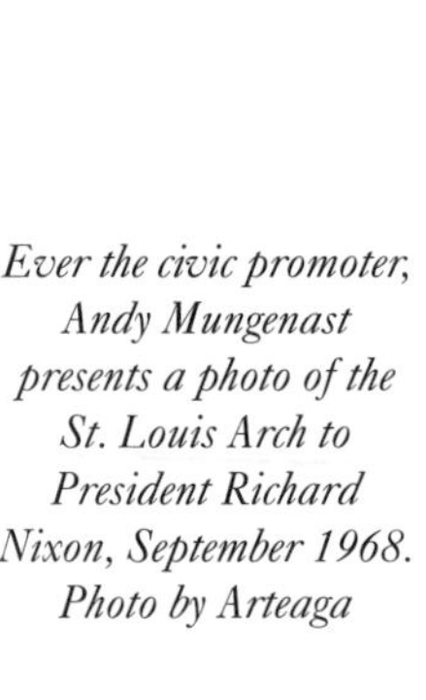

Ever the civic promoter, Andy Mungenast presents a photo of the St. Louis Arch to President Richard Nixon, September 1968. Photo by Arteaga

He explained, "From the very first, our idea was to sell St. Louis to St. Louisans. All that people were doing in those days was apologizing, saying we had lousy climate, we had smoke, this was wrong, that was wrong. We set out to boost St. Louis."

One of Mungenast's ideas for boosting St. Louis was a program that placed several hundred historical markers on spots throughout the city and county. In his capacity as a patriarch of the Jaycees and a tireless booster for St. Louis, Mungenast also served as an official greeter for the City, and in that capacity became friends with Charles Lindbergh, Admiral Richard Byrd, Jimmy Doolittle, and other celebrities of the era, and on one occasion met President Richard Nixon. Andy Mungenast never ceased working, either at his job or for the community. He officially retired from Streckfus at the age of 80. In a celebration held at the home of Captain Bill Streckfus, the Captain thanked and congratulated Andy for his service, then said, "I suppose we will see you bright and early in the morning." Sure enough, the Streckfus people sent a car each morning to pick up Andy who would spend a few hours at the boat, then be returned home by early afternoon. He died the following June.

Charlotte Mungenast welcomes President George W.H. Bush to a Jaycees convention.

When Andrew died in 1976, he was the nation's oldest living Jaycee, having held the title of "Permanent Honorary President" for decades. Like her husband, Charlotte Mungenast also believed in service to the community. She served as president of the St. Louis University High School Mother's Club, and in the 1970s she was a founder and first president of the Shrewsbury, Missouri chapter of the American Association of Retired Persons. She was beloved among the Jaycees, was given the title of "Honorary First Lady of the International Junior Chamber of Commerce," and was faithfully invited to its conventions, even after

Andy's death. She held that title until she died in late November, 1991. Today, the organization is based in Tulsa, Oklahoma, where a campaign was begun in the early 1990s to create the Andrew and Charlotte Mungenast Memorial Library, where the archives and historical artifacts of the Jaycees are housed. That institution, honoring the work of its namesakes, was dedicated on January 16, 1993.

When Charlotte Mungenast died in 1991, the Mungenasts of St. Louis had grown to a clan with 30 grandchildren and 28 great-grandchildren. Andrew and Charlotte left high standards for their children to live up to as responsible members of the community. This they have done, but for some time it appeared that David, their fourth son, was going to fall woefully short of the mark.

CHAPTER TWO

Dave Mungenast: The Troublesome Gift

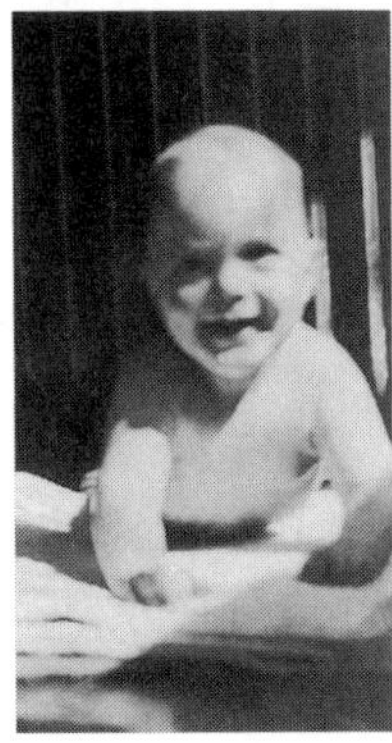

David Frances Mungenast, age one.

Andrew and Charlotte Mungenast produced six children. They included Andrew, Thomas, John, and Charlotte P., all born between 1924 and 1930. Then came Dave and Carl, born in 1934 and 1940 respectively. Andy Mungenast, Jr. recalls, "Mother had the first four children, and with John she was declared dead of a heart attack during delivery. She was revived, but it was a long period of time before she had David and Carl." David was only 8 and Carl was only 2 when their elder brother Andy went into the military and to service in World War II. No one may have realized it at the time, but the difference was not just the passage of time between and first and second groups of the Mungenast children. The first four, and the second two respectively, were born on opposite sides of a cultural watershed in American history. Though brought up in the same household as Andy, John, Charlotte P., and Thomas, David and Carl experienced their formative years in a world that had been radically altered by the Second World War. A new economy driven by consumerism and easy credit had begun. Women, drawn into the workplace by wartime defense requirements, were finding it difficult to return to their traditional role, especially since the men they knew had returned from war changed and restless, or had not returned at all. Fear of communism and nuclear conflagration, trumpeted constantly by the government and the press, took hold across the land. And a new internal menace—the juvenile delinquent—was threatening society to the extent that Senator Estes Kefauver and others conducted an investigation to explore the origins of a supposed wave of crime, violence, and rebellion among America's youth. Indeed, it may have been the same household at 3940 Connecticut Street where Andrew and Charlotte raised all six of their children, but during the process, the world around them had changed.

Dave Mungenast recalls, "I remember the first time I heard the term 'juvenile delinquent.' We were around the dinner table and my father was talking about the changes brought on by the war. He talked about the fact that in many families both parents were working. Children were spending much of their days with little parental supervision. Their social center was no longer their family, but their peers, whom they met at favorite hangouts in the community. Dad did not like what he saw happening, and he predicted that juvenile delinquency would become a blight on society."

To the consternation of Andrew and Charlotte Mungenast, the new breed of post-war American youth, seen as quite troubling at the time, emerged in their own son, David. Raised in a strict Catholic environment, all of the children attended Holy Family parochial school in South St. Louis. Subsequently, the boys attended St. Louis University High School, a Jesuit-run college preparatory institution, and Charlotte attended St. Elizabeth's Academy. Both were schools with high academic standards, necessary to the kind of upbringing expected in the Mungenast household. Virginia Mungenast, who lived in the neighborhood and married Tom, recalls, "All of the older children were very good students, and the first three boys were all 'goody two-shoes' types. It was like they could do no wrong. With Dave and Carl it was different. Especially for Dave, who became the black sheep of the family."

As a youngster, Dave Mungenast dreamed of being a mountaineer, living off the land. He subscribed to *Fir, Fish, and Game*, bought other outdoor magazines, and dreamed of living in a cabin in Alaska. He read "Call of the Wild" and thought about what it was like living in the 18th and 19th centuries. He enjoyed going to the territorial old court house downtown where the slave Dred Scott first pled his case. Now a museum and historical land-

David, approximately age nine, with his sister Charlotte Patricia.

David Mungenast, age 12.

mark, it displayed fascinating and instructive dioramas of the early days of the Louisiana Purchase when trappers and traders moved their booty up and down the Mississippi. He recalls, "My grandfather had a place about 12 miles away on the Mississippi River. I would go there on weekends to hunt and trap. I could catch fish, gut them, and make a stew, then boil my traps in it to eliminate any trace of human scent. I learned how to scrape and salt the hides of the animals I caught, and I would bring them back to St. Louis to sell to the Taylor Fur Company." It was a happy time for the youngster whose friends nicknamed him "Trapper Dave." "My outdoors activities kept me out in the woods and out of trouble." However, his dreams of the solitary life of a Mountain Man began to change in the summer of his 16th year when he got a job

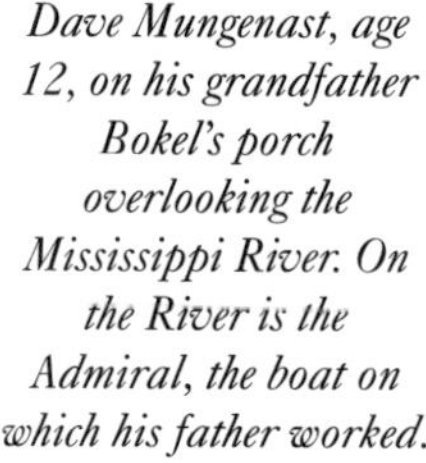
Dave Mungenast, age 12, on his grandfather Bokel's porch overlooking the Mississippi River. On the River is the Admiral, the boat on which his father worked.

tending and wrangling horses at a Catholic girl's camp. Reflecting the opinion of many young men of 16, he says, "I decided there might be something to this girl thing." David's life began to change.

Unlike his older siblings, Dave Mungenast failed to excel at school, but it was not for a lack of intellect. He says, "I was great at arithmetic. I could have the answers to problems before the teacher finished writing them on the board. I was fair in English and history, about 85 percentile. But I got in trouble for being a wise guy in class. I mouthed off and even challenged the priests and nuns about theological issues." It did not help matters that the nuns and priests were always ready to tell him what gems his older brothers had been, and how he would never amount to anything. Still, he knew that education was very important in his family, and that he was expected to attend St. Louis University High School, just like his older brothers had. He says, "I placed well on the entrance exams and started in a highly-ranked class, but that didn't last long." As if his poor attitude toward school did not cause problems enough, Mungenast missed a lot of his first high school year recuperating from an appendectomy. He says, "When I returned I was way behind, and I just went backwards

Dave, age 14, upon graduation from Holy Family Parochial School.

from there, ending up in the lowest ranked class." He was asked by the Jesuits not to return the following year, essentially kicked out of the school where other Mungenast siblings had done the family proud.

Dave enrolled the following year in Roosevelt High School, a public school. He says, "After three years with the Jesuits, it was easy, and I didn't have to study. I set a record for cutting the most days of school. I would call in sick, or sometimes when my dad dropped me off in front of the school I would walk right through the building and out the back door. I would go downtown where there were movie theaters offering a double feature for 15 cents, and I would buy a dozen doughnuts and spend the day watching movies. Sometimes a bunch of us guys would cut school and go swimming. We never got away with it. I would be told to report to the principal's office the next day, and there would be all the guys I went swimming with. At dinner my father would ask me how school went. I would get caught in a lie because he knew I had skipped before he asked me."

To make the situation even worse, Dave discovered motorcycles, and at the age of 16 he and a friend pitched in to buy a used 1946 Indian Chief for $100. The venture didn't last long when Mungenast wrecked the bike on his way home from purchasing it. He says, "My parents never knew about it. I returned the crashed bike to its owner, my buddy got his money back, and I walked away with nothing." His next bike was a somewhat smaller Indian, a converted WWII military model. Next came a 1950 British BSA set up for off-road riding. On this bike Mungenast began to enter off-road endurance competitions, finding a joy of riding and learning the skills that would eventually form a purpose in his life and lead him into world-class competition. In 1953, at the age of 19, Mungenast bought his first new motorcycle, a BSA Gold Star, considered at that time the state of the art in performance and design.

Undoubtedly, David's interest in motorcycling was seen as just another example of his incorrigible slide into juvenile delinquency. Motorcycles were not the fashionable toy of the affluent they have become for many today. They were associated with danger, disrespect for authority, and youthful rebellion, all of which was burned into the American psyche with the release of the motion picture, "The Wild One," starring Marlon Brando, which began to appear in theaters across the nation the same year that Mungenast bought his new BSA Gold Star. Dave and his friends fit the image depicted by the movie, riding their bikes, hanging out, and wearing jeans, engineer boots, and white T-shirts, sometimes with cigarettes rolled up in the sleeve. Eventually, this image would be romanticized into a kind of American folk hero, caricatured by Paul LeMat as John Milner in the 1973 film "American Graffiti" and made comic by Henry Winkler as Arthur Fonzarelli in its small screen spin-off "Happy Days" in 1974. But it was 1953, and these were not happy days for the Mungenast family. David was not following a straight and narrow path, and sometimes deliberately provoking his parents and teachers. To the chagrin of his mother, he wrote crude words on his motorcycle helmet. On another occasion he stole a photo-

Dave with the so-called Dirty Dozen. A cast on his broken arm is visible below his jacket sleeve.

graph of an attractive woman from his brother Andy's album from his travels in the military, and showed it around the neighborhood, claiming that he was engaged to a dancer at a strip club on Broadway.

Dave aboard his BSA Gold Star, riding with a cast on his broken right arm.

At Roosevelt High School, Dave met Ron and Gene Huch, and other young men his age involved with motorcycles, and they formed a group that called itself, self-importantly, "The Dirty Dozen." Wayne DeWitt, a member of the group and a lifelong friend of Dave's, jokes about the Dirty Dozen, "I think there were seven of us." Huch recalls, "Dave was always on the wild side. Most of us had a crew cut. Dave had a ducktail." About their rowdy behavior, Huch explains, "We were always just marginally legal. Most of our motorcycles were always falling apart. They had loud pipes or were not properly equipped or licensed for the street, and we would often attract the attention of the police. We would run from the cops, and one of our favorite tricks was to head for Tower Grove Park where we would jump the curb and ride right into the park, then we would scatter in all directions, knowing that most or all of us would get away." He continues, "One time Dave fled, sped down the alley behind his house, and pulled into his back yard. His mother had hung out the laundry, so he pulled his BSA in behind the sheets on the line and hid there for about a half an hour. When he came out, there was a motorcycle cop sitting in the alley, waiting for him. But Dave managed to talk his way out of it because the cop really could not be certain that he was one of the guys they had chased earlier."

Not surprisingly, Dave Mungenast was short of the credits necessary to graduate from Roosevelt High School, and was required to go to night classes at Hadley Vo-tech School where he finally earned enough credits for his high school diploma. At Hadley he completed a psychology class by only reading the book. With his teacher's permission, he never attended class, but passed his final exam, proving once and for all that his motivational problems in school had never been due to a lack of intelligence. By then he was holding down a fulltime job, driving a parts delivery truck for Roberts Chevrolet. His predecessor in the job had spent the whole day picking up or delivering parts. Mungenast says, "First thing in the morning I would look at my deliveries and carefully plan my route. I would work everything out so I could end up at Bob Schultz's motorcycle shop about noon. I would have lunch there and hang out a while, then be back at Roberts by 2 p.m. with my work all done. They were just amazed that I could finish so early, and they had no idea I had been goofing off for the last couple of hours at the motorcycle shop." This logical approach to planning, organizing, and creating systems would later become one of the basic ingredients for Dave Mungenast's success in business. Still, at the time, he had no aspirations and no plans except hanging out with his motorcycling friends. He recalls, "When my parents would raise the subject of my future, I would say something like, 'I don't know. Maybe I'll just keep driving a truck,' just to get a reaction out of them."

Today, the Mungenast men are reluctant to talk in much detail about their teenage years. Dave's younger brother Carl says that there were many "incidents" when he or Dave ended up on the wrong side of the law. He says, "Fortunately, we never got into really serious trouble, and there were times when we really deserved to. People in the neighborhood knew how religious our father was, and our scrapes with the law became kind of a neighborhood joke. We would do something bad and get off, and everyone would say, 'Well, it looks like ol' Andy's prayers paid off again.'" Looking back, Mungenast says, "I went down some wrong paths, but I am glad that my parents lived long enough to see it all work out."

The Mungenasts were a deeply religious family who believed that God has a plan and that everything is for a reason. Reflecting on how troublesome Dave had become, and how he differed so much from his older brothers who were superb students and upstanding boys who filled their civic-minded parents with pride, Charlotte Mungenast would say, "Dave was a gift from God to keep me from feeling too high and mighty." It was a theological explanation that likely provided her little real comfort at the time.

CHAPTER THREE

Green Beret: In Service to Country, In Discovery of Self

Dave Mungenast, Green Beret, 1955.

Barbara McAboy was raised in South St. Louis, just on the opposite side of Tower Grove Park from the Mungenast neighborhood, yet she grew up in a culture that was different from the German Catholic and Lutheran environment on the south side of the park. Four years Dave's junior, she was raised with older and younger sisters in a Baptist family of Scots/Irish and French parentage. Her mother could trace her lineage back to the early French colonists who settled the Louisiana Territory south of St. Louis. Barbara was an energetic and self-reliant young woman who ran with a popular crowd, evidenced by the fact that she was rushed to join the Omega Sigma Lambda sorority at Roosevelt High School.

The same day that Barbara was initiated into Omega Sigma Lambda, Dave Mungenast performed the hare-brained stunt of stepping off the back bumper of a buddy's speeding 1934 Plymouth, ending up with a broken arm. Barbara says, "He had a reputation as a pretty rowdy guy. He was not a big trouble-maker or fighter, but still the other guys knew not to mess with him. He hung out with motorcycle buddies who called themselves The Dirty Dozen." Still, Barbara must have found his dangerous reputation exciting, because she made the first move. She recalls, "One evening my girlfriends and I were going to Mary Ann's Ice Cream Parlor at the corner of Grand and Shenandoah. This was our hangout, just like the drive-in in 'American Graffiti.' There was Dave, standing there in his tight jeans with a ducktail haircut and his arm in a cast. He was tall and good looking, and I walked up to him and said, 'Hi!'" Barbara's friend, Carol Fisher, helped arrange their first date, which was a hayride sponsored by their sorority. Later she would confess to her father, "I know this guy is not good for me, Dad, but . . ."

In the opening scene of "American Graffiti," in the parking lot of Mel's Drive-in, Steve Bolander says to Curt Henderson, "You can't stay seventeen forever." At the age of 20, Dave Mungenast began to come to a similar conclusion. He was working at Roberts Chevrolet and riding motorcycles when news broke that on January 31, 1955, the government intended to do away with the G.I. Bill under which so many young veterans had gotten an education and their start in post-WWII America. Dave had entered St. Louis University in September, 1954. He says, "Dad got me admitted, and I don't know how he did it, but I was not off to a good start." His old habits were surfacing and Dave was failing. He says, "I hated school, but had begun to realize I might need a better education. I knew the only way I could afford to do that in the future might be through military service and the G.I. Bill. I told the school that if they would give me a WP (withdrew while passing) before my grades got any worse, I would leave and join the military. His teachers agreed, and Dave went to enlist. In the process of exploring his options, Mungenast learned that becoming Airborne qualified paid an extra $55 a month, which would provide compensation of a total of $140 a month. He says, "It was as simple as that. I didn't have any idea what I was getting into, but it paid more and that is what mattered, so I joined the Special Forces where I would learn jumping and underwater demolition." Military service put his relationship with Barbara on hiatus. She recalls, "I was a senior in high school when he went to Korea. We decided we should date other people while he was gone, so that's what we did."

Dave during Special Forces survival training in Colorado.

Mungenast was sent first to Fort Chaffee in Arkansas for eight weeks of basic training. From there he went to Camp Jackson in South Carolina for eight weeks of light infantry, then to jump school at Fort Benning in Georgia. Later, when Dave was ordered to Fort Hale in Colorado for Special Forces winter mountaineering and survival training, circumstances were such that his older brother Andy, a pilot, could fly him out from St. Louis in a B25 bomber. Andy says, "As we were coming in on final approach, I looked over at Dave and he looked scared to death. I said, 'What's the matter? Haven't you flown before?' and Dave said, 'Yes, I've been up over a dozen times, but this is my first landing!'"

After Fort Benning it was on to Fort Bragg for Special Forces training where he became a specialist in explosives and underwater demolition. Dave explains, "One of the roles of the Special Forces is to send in teams to train indigenous people the techniques of guerilla warfare so they can create a resistance force that is as disruptive as possible." During an exercise called Operation Tropic Dolphin, Dave's team was working with a group of troops who spoke only Spanish. He recalls, "I knew little Spanish and was trying to show them how to arm a bomb, using only gestures. Well, it didn't go off, so there I was trying to show them how to disarm a live explosive with only gestures." He laughs, "I can tell you I worked up a sweat! That kind of experience helps build character." During Operation Sagebrush, Dave played the opposite role, masquerading in civilian clothing for

Dave during airborne training.

three weeks in Louisiana with the mission of disrupting U.S. military exercises.

On one occasion at Fort Hale during night skiing training, one of Dave's squad broke his leg, and Dave had to pull him five or six miles to safety aboard a sled. On another occasion, Dave says, "We had eaten snake and poke leaves, and were ready for something different. I used a small explosive charge to kill fish in a lake. As they came to the surface, we paddled around in a rubber boat and scooped them up with our hats." He smiles as he recalls, "There was one guy so hungry that he didn't even bother to clean the fish. He poked a stick down its throat, cooked it for two or three minutes over the fire, then tried to eat it like corn on the cob, innards and all." It must have been a highly entertaining sight to a man like Dave, who had learned all about catching and cleaning fish and game when he was still just a

Thirteen take-offs and no landings. Airborne Dave is the second man from the left.

Dave posing with a Russian MIG 15 in Korea.

young boy visiting his grandfather's home on the Mississippi River.

Upon completing his training, Dave got lucky. Most of his friends were shipped to Okinawa, then on to Vietnam. Dave was deployed to Korea where he drew Honor Guard duty, serving as a body guard for high-ranking officers and visiting diplomats. He explains, "It was kind of the Army's version of the Secret Service." It must have been a broadening experience for a young man who had spent most of his life in South St. Louis, because he was quartered with a United Nations platoon that included troops from Thailand, Korea, Australia, Turkey, and other countries supporting the UN peacekeeping mission. While in Korea, Dave got involved with men from his unit who supported a local orphanage. Fellow Honor Guardsman Bob Neblett recalls, "Those of us who volunteered to get involved were asked to write home to our friends and churches to solicit donations to the orphanage. Dave got tremendous results. It was obvious that he had influence with a very big network of people who cared." This was Mungenast's first taste of philanthropic work on behalf of young people, and it would later become a major undertaking in his life.

Those who knew Dave before and after his military service readily comment on how much it matured him. However, maturity did not arrive overnight. Even after training there remained the cut-up behavior that had caused Dave so much difficulty in high school. Neblett tells of the time when Mungenast was assigned as personal body guard to a General. He recounts, "Dave

Honor Guard, Korea.

On leave in Hong Kong.

was in a jeep, following the General's car as they sped by. We were marching and he was driving and decided to rub it in. As he went by he turned to us with a big silly grin and was waving to us, not watching where he was going." The General's car stopped abruptly and Dave rammed his jeep into the back of it, knocking the General's wife onto the floor. Neblett continues, "Dave rushed to the General's wife and opened the door to help her up, and began apologizing profusely, expressing great concern for her wellbeing. The General was furious. He climbed out of the car and stormed around to the other side to take Dave apart. But by the time he got there, Dave had so charmed the General's wife that she ordered him to leave the poor boy alone. He had only made an honest mistake and there was no harm done." The General calmed down and Dave escaped without punishment. This ability to establish a sincere rapport with others under difficult circumstances was a skill that would serve Mungenast well throughout his business career.

It was in the Special Forces where Dave's leadership ability and style began to emerge. Dr. Frank Falero first met Mungenast at Special Forces training at Fort Bragg, after which they went separate ways, then ended up together again as Honor Guardsmen in Korea. Falero, who later earned a PhD in Economics and became a professor and advisor to government officials and congressmen, recalls, "I was a kid who came from a tough New York

Dave's work in philanthropy began when members of the 8th Army Division provided support to young Korean orphans. Dave is second from the right.

neighborhood, and my life was not going in a good direction. I look back, realize that Mungie [this is what his military comrades called Mungenast] had a big influence on what I became and later accomplished. He was only a couple of years older than me, but he was a role model. He never lost his temper and he never did anything stupid. He was always in control. We went out and had a good time, but he never behaved in a way that would give him something to apologize for the next day. Being around him taught me behavior that became very beneficial in my life." Falero adds, "He never told me what to do or how to act, but he instructed by example." Falero's recollection of this leadership style is consistent with what many of Mungenast's associates will tell one today; that Dave leads by example.

Mustering out with an honorable discharge in December, 1957, David returned to St. Louis a different man. He says, "Special Forces training is a great confidence builder." His motorcycle buddy and lifelong friend Dave Larsen says, "The military taught Dave how to focus; to look at his options and decide what is important." Former hell-raising companion and Dirty Dozen member Ron Huch says, "Dave came back from the army a much more mature guy." Mungenast adds, "The stuff your parents tried to beat into you, it finally takes hold. It is all there, even if you don't think it is, and gradually it begins to make sense. As you get older, your parents get smarter." Dave got a job as a mechanic at Bob Schultz's motorcycle store in January, 1958. He began to see Barbara again and enrolled in St. Louis University the following September under the G.I. Bill. He married Barbara on January 24, 1959, and completed his degree in geography and anthropology in three years while carrying a full-time job. Barbara recalls, "He maintained a horrendous schedule. He was very organized and always had a dozen things going at once. The day we got married, he wore his tuxedo pants to school because he had to complete an exam and rush right to the wedding."

About his course of study, Dave explains, "At first I majored in psychology and business management. I thought that psychology would teach me more about understanding people. The first class was about nothing but rats. I went to the teacher after class and asked if this is what psychology is all about. Rats! She explained how important the study of rats was to understanding the human mind, and I said, 'Ma'am, I'm not sure I'm the right guy to be a psychology major.' I learned that it was not too late to transfer, and I changed my majors to geography and anthropology. I had always been interested in geography, and I figured anthropology would teach me more about people than studying rats."

After graduation Dave got a job at the Aeronautical Chart and Information Center in St. Louis, making maps. Years later, in a radio interview that touched on his unlikely education in the course of becoming a successful St. Louis businessman, Mungenast joked, "You know how hard it is to fold a map? Well, I can do that!" At the same time, Mungenast continued to work as a mechanic at Bob Schultz's motorcycle store, maintaining two jobs and a new marriage. Schultz was traveling a lot and had opened a second store, and for all intents and purposes, Dave was continuing his work as a mechanic while functioning as a general manager for the store. He says, "Barbara and I didn't have much, but the two jobs were really not necessary. I just had that much drive and energy, and I really loved being involved with motorcycles." Barbara agrees, "Dave is a driven man. He always has been. I still am not sure what drives him, but he is always busy and always looking for new opportunities." To further complicate their busy lives, their first son, David, Jr. arrived on April 1, 1960. The young couple had been living with Dave's parents, and with the arrival of a new child, the lack of privacy became a less than healthy situation. Dave and Barbara rented a small apartment, then Ray was born on July 17, 1961. The following year they built a house at Lake Montowese, south of St. Louis.

In "American Graffiti," Curt Henderson is a young man who believes he is not ready to grow up. He has an opportunity to travel back East for college, but thinks maybe he would rather hang around home and enjoy himself. Throughout the movie he is haunted by fleeting appearances of a mysterious blonde woman in a white Thunderbird. She is rumored to be a prostitute or someone's wife. Curt becomes obsessed with pursuing her, but over a single, chaotic night at Mel's Drive-In and while cruising the strip, he begins to see the world as an adult. In the final scene of the movie, Curt is on an airplane, flying away toward college and his future. Through the window of the airplane he can see the white Thunderbird, traveling down the highway, far beneath him. The blonde in the Thunderbird becomes a small and disappearing symbol of his irresponsible, youthful past. While Dave still pursued risk, excitement, and his dreams of adventure through his off-road riding and motorcycle racing activities, by 1962 there appeared to be little remaining of the young delinquent who had confounded his parents and earned notoriety by getting expelled from one school after another. Training as a Green Beret, marriage, a growing family, and hard work at which he found personal enjoyment had done what priests and nuns had failed to do. Dave Mungenast, it seems, had begun to view the world through the eyes of an adult.

CHAPTER FOUR

A Passion for Motorcycles: Dave Gets Down to Business

The 1960s were a very special decade. It was a time of change and revolution. A chaotic youth movement was taking place throughout the United States and Europe. The Vietnam War divided America and erased much of the national confidence that had emerged from the triumph of the Second World War. Changes in music, fashion, mores, and family structure all heralded an upheaval in society, and it concentrated itself in the Baby Boomers, the largest generation and most affluent middle class that America had ever produced. Revolution and change could be seen even in the public's attitude toward motorcycles. The decade began with the image imprinted by the mid-50s motion picture "The Wild One," depicting motorcyclists as an underclass of thugs and shiftless rebels. No self-respecting person wanted to have anything to do with motorcycles. "Easy Rider," released in 1969, presented a more sympathetic yet enigmatic image. Peter Fonda's Captain America was no longer a man who terrorized small towns; rather, he sought only to be free, and it was the dark side of America's "traditional values" that terrorized him. He vividly symbolized the youth movement of the decade, and his chopper became in iconic image that symbolized a new generation's love affair with motorcycles.

Dave Mungenast's love affair with motorcycles was long established by the time the Boomers discovered bikes. He had ridden one since 1950 and become a skilled off-road rider, he had helped form the Midwest Enduro Team—a legitimate sport-oriented club—in 1953, and he had been making a living at a motorcycle dealership since 1958, performing a diverse range of duties from mechanic to sales to general management. Bob Schultz, Dave's boss, remembers, "He was very dedicated to making a financial success for himself and his young wife. He became nearly indispensable to me. When I opened a second store I was confident that my original shop would be in good hands with Dave as its general manager. He was an excellent mechanic and top-notch at dealing with people. He was absolutely dependable and always did what he said he would do." Schultz adds, "I never thought of Dave as an employee. I thought of him as an associate and a good friend. I think that attitude produced good results." Indeed, Bob Schultz pioneered the concept of the "motorcycle supermarket," changing the retail environment from grubby one-brand storefronts to a stand-alone big box structure with many brands and a vast and colorful array of accessories.

To a large extent, America's changing attitude toward motorcycles was driven by changes in the motorcycle itself. By the late 1950s, a new kind of motorcycle was coming from a Japanese company named Honda. It was smaller, quieter, less intimidating, easier to ride, and far more reliable than traditional American and British motorcycles. Hondas carried electric starters as standard equipment years before other brands even began to understand their importance to a new, expanding customer base of middle-class Americans. Hondas were built with such quality and to such close tolerances that they did not leak oil to soil the clothes or driveways of their owners. Audaciously, the company promoted its product with a slogan that would have seemed laughable if applied to traditional brands, such as Triumph or Harley-Davidson: "You meet the nicest people on a Honda" became the company's declaration about its product and its clientele. Most importantly, the dollar-yen relationship at the time made Hondas an incredible bargain to Americans interested in trying their hand at motorcycling for the first time. Still, they were Japanese, and at the dawn of the 1960s, many Americans had a post-war prejudice against the Japanese race and a belief that they could build only ticky-tacky and derivative junk.

Bob Schultz recalls, "I first saw a picture of a Honda in a magazine that a friend in the Service brought back from Japan. I wrote to Honda and they sent me a big set of engineering drawings. It was a curious response, but I suppose they had no English language promotional literature at that time." In the meantime, Dave Mungenast had been in touch with Ron Huch, a long-time friend who had moved from St. Louis to the West Coast. Huch had been hanging around the motorcycle shop of the legendary racer Bud Ekins where he saw some of the first Hondas to arrive in the United States. Huch spoke highly of the design and quality of the little-known Japanese product, and Dave passed those claims on to Bob Schultz, encouraging him to bring Honda into his product line. Schultz had a very painful memory that may have influenced his decision to take the plunge. A few years earlier a man had pitched him on a new kind of car coming out of Germany, but Bob decided that no one in his right mind would want to buy a rear-engine, air-cooled automobile as small and ugly as the Volkswagen. He was loath to make that mistake a second time, so he placed an order, becoming one of the first motorcycle dealers in America to order a batch of Hondas, even before the company's American distributorship had been formally established in Gardena, California. It proved an inauspicious beginning. The motorcycles that showed up were pink, and their carburetors were jetted improperly for American fuel. Mungenast says, "Every one of them burned pistons, and I had to rebuild them all."

But Honda is a company that confronts and overcomes problems quickly, and it wasted little time adapting to the demands of the American market. In the late 1950s, between 40,000 and 50,000 motorcycles per year were sold in the United States, including all domestic and imported brands. Honda alone sold 17,000 units its first year of business in America. A motorcycle sales boom had begun, and Yamaha, Suzuki, Kawasaki, and other brands flowed out of Japan as well. Europe still had a thriving motorcycle industry, so the Boomers wishing to throw a leg over a motorcycle were gifted with a vast choice of various sizes and styles of motorcycles. Mungenast wanted a stake in the game, not just a weekly paycheck. Schultz valued his talents and began to negotiate a partnership. Schultz appraised and valued his business at $50,000, so asked $25,000 to bring Dave in as a full partner. Dave could not come close to raising that much cash, so he decided to strike out on his own, winning a Honda franchise to open a store at 6820 Gravois in South St. Louis, some ten miles

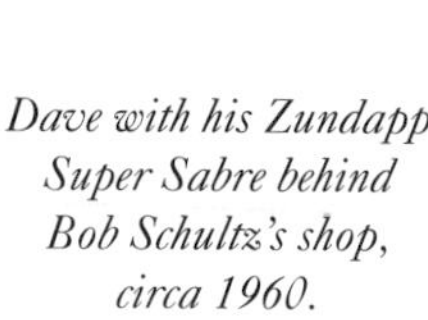

Dave with his Zundapp Super Sabre behind Bob Schultz's shop, circa 1960.

from Schultz's downtown Locust Street location. The move was made with Bob Schultz's blessing, and the two remained lifelong friends. Schultz says, "I never thought of him as a competitor. We had similar views about how to do business. We believed that you get customers by how you treat them, not by trying to steal them from another dealer."

In preparation for opening his new shop, Mungenast hired 19-year-old Dave Larsen, whom he had met in 1962 when he sold him a Triumph motorcycle at Schultz's. Like many Schultz customers, Larsen hung around the shop and became friends with Dave. Even while Mungenast was finishing his last months at Schultz's in late 1964, Larsen was working at the new shop on Gravois, preparing for its official opening on January 1, 1965. St. Louis Honda's first order was for 20 motorcycles, some special tools, and sales materials, amounting to an outlay of $7,524.75, borrowed from Security Trust Company of St. Louis. Those 20 motorcycles lasted no time at all. Larsen recalls, "There were never more than four employees, and we moved a thousand motorcycles that first year! They were going out the door as fast as we could uncrate and prep them for sale. We would prep the bikes at night, and they would be all gone the next day. We worked nine to nine five days a week and nine to six on Saturday,

Dave and Pat O'Mara at Bob Schultz's dealership where Dave worked as a mechanic in 1964.

and we loved every minute of it. It was a fun and exciting business." Others on the original team were the brothers Dick and Pat O'Mara. Dick became service manager and Pat worked in the evenings, setting up bikes and doing what needed to be done.

Motorcycles were hot in 1965, but no little measure of St. Louis Honda's early success was due to the personal qualities and business philosophy of Dave Mungenast. As an employer, he worked more as a colleague and role model than a boss. Larsen says, "Dave is pretty damned good at anything he tries, and when you were learning something, he was right there learning it along

The way it used to be. Cloth riding gear, open face helmet, and duct tape around the leg. Dave riding a Czechoslovakian CZ competition motorcycle.

with you. If he already knew what needed to be done, he was a good teacher. He didn't send us out to unload a truck. He came along and unloaded it with us. Dave has a good ability to find someone's strong suit, then encourage them in that direction. I have never seen him push someone into a job they couldn't do." Larsen adds, "He is an inspirational employer, and this is not something he learned at a management seminar. It is just natural Dave."

As a salesman, Dave Mungenast found his true voice. Larsen explains, "He has a unique conversational ability that enables

Dave wins the 1964 Riverdale Speedway Marathon and a national championship for Honda. With Dave are Pat O'Mara and Jim Hardie.

him to get very close to people in a short period of time. He would ask people what part of town they were from or what school they went to. He could always connect with them on a personal level." Then Larsen laughs, "Maybe that was because he went to all of those schools himself!" "Seriously," Larsen continues, "He listens and can make people comfortable. He does not start pushing product, but tries to discover what their interests are so he can suggest the product they need. As a result, our customers were not just buying Honda motorcycles. They were buying motorcycles from Dave Mungenast because they trusted him, and, over time, that trust turned into many repeat sales and some lifetime customers." Mungenast's ability to listen has become one of the fundamental principles upon which he has built his success. He calls this principle "The Platinum Rule." He explains, "You have heard of the Golden Rule: 'Do unto others as you would have them do unto you.' Well, the Platinum Rule takes that to another level of customer service. You don't treat others the way *YOU* want to be treated. You treat them the way *THEY* want to be treated. Of course, you have to really listen and try to understand them and really understand what they want before you can apply The Platinum Rule."

Customer service became the foundation on which Dave Mungenast has built all of his retail businesses. Larsen explains, "He never wanted anyone to be unhappy with him or with the store. He was selling a lot of bikes to friends from school and from the neighborhood, and he wanted to keep them as friends. He also believed that a happy customer would be a future customer, and that good word-of-mouth is the best way to make the business grow. While we did not compromise on price, we offered customers better service than anyone else." Dick O'Mara concurs, "Dave would bend over backwards for people even when he shouldn't have, just because he wanted the store to have a good reputation. Sometimes customers took advantage of that, and Dave would go their way even when he knew we had not caused a problem." O'Mara recalls an example: "I remember a guy who came in with damage on his bike and said we did it in the service department. I knew it was not true, and I said to him, 'Look, we're going to fix this at no charge because that's how Mr. Mungenast does things, but just between you and me, we both know you're lying!'" O'Mara smiles and adds, "He got satisfaction, but he never tried that stuff on us again." Over time, Dave Mungenast would begin to think of his customers as "clients." He explains, "I never want to sell anyone one of anything. I want them to come back again and again. So I encourage my employees to think in terms of dealing with clients whom we hope to continue to serve over a long period of time."

With business booming, Dave acquired a Triumph franchise toward the end of 1965. Triumph, a traditional British brand, was larger and far more powerful than the Hondas of the era. It appealed to a more rugged and sporting riders, or to individuals who had become confident on their little Hondas and wanted to move up to something more powerful. Dave Larsen explains, "It was a good move for a shop seeking return business. People would buy a little 90cc or 160cc Honda. Then they would come back to trade it for a larger 250cc or 305cc Honda. And some would continue the process with the purchase of a 500cc or 650cc

Dave conducts a drawing for a free motorcycle at the grand opening of his Honda dealership in 1965.

Triumph. Then the 750cc Honda Four arrived on the scene. As customers got older or grew more committed to motorcycling, we had a more exciting product they could move up to." Business was so good that Mungenast bought out a Honda dealership in St. Charles, Missouri, dispatching Pat O'Mara to manage the store. But a dark period lay just ahead. Boom time in the motorcycle business was about to come to an end.

Dave Mungenast's personal inclination toward off-road motorcycling flavored the development of the small enterprise. Although he sold Honda and Triumph street machines, there was definitely an inclination at St. Louis Honda toward the sporting and competition side of motorcycling. Dave and others on the staff were active competitors who entered local enduros and the occasional race on Sundays, and the shop served as a home base for the Midwest Enduro Team. Other brands with sporting models were brought into the product mix, such as the German Zundapp or Hercules, then later the Swedish Husqvarna and Austrian-built, American-designed Penton were added to the line of off-road and racing machines available to customers. Eventually the interest in motor sports would be incorporated into the name of the business.

Healthy sales were driven by credit, and Dave established a good relationship with John Tacke of Gravois Bank, an independent neighborhood establishment that dated back to the 1880s. Tacke says, "In those days you could lend money on somebody's character. You did not have to secure the loan with 100% collateral. I visited the store often to see how it was going, and I got to see how Dave dealt with his customers. Over a lifetime of banking, you maybe meet five or ten people you can totally rely on, and Dave is one of them. I don't remember ever hearing a lie from Dave, and I never saw him speak to another person abusively." Tacke became a living example of Dave's business success through fair dealing and good customer service. Tacke and several of his colleagues eventually bought Honda Scramblers from St. Louis Honda, then over the next three decades he and members of his immediate family bought more than twenty automobiles from Mungenast's various dealerships. In return, Mungenast stayed with Tacke as his main banker for 35 years, even after Gravois Bank had been swallowed up in a series of mergers and acquisitions that has become the ever-changing

Dave Mungenast and his staff at the 6820 Gravois store in 1966. Left to right: David Tufts, Andrew Mungenast (Dave's nephew), Bruce Bogue, Dick O'Mara, Dave Mungenast, Bob Mullins, Carlo Martellaro, Bob Franklin, and Pat O'Mara. Dave Larsen is away on active duty in the Army Reserve.

World motocross champion Torsten Hallman visits Dave's store on the occasion of his becoming a Husqvarna dealer.

landscape of American banking. But, good relationships notwithstanding, Vietnam and the draft stepped into the mix, causing a precipitous decline in motorcycle sales in 1967. Dave Larsen explains, "The bottom dropped out in 1968. So many young men were being called up by the draft, it became standard practice for loan applications to include a space for Selective Service Status. When a guy wrote down '1A' it was all over. No loan for him!"

Looking back, Mungenast says, "During my first twenty years in business, it was one crisis after another. I didn't have an opportunity to manage a business because I was always scrambling to stay afloat." At one point Mungenast even had to seek a loan from his employee, Dave Larsen. Larsen offered his life savings of $7,500, just to help keep the doors open. It turned out to be a good investment, because years later Mungenast would buy back Larsen's share for better than 50 times its initial value, and Larsen still remains with the Mungenast organization today as its most senior employee, the only man at Dave's side from the very beginning. But at the time it must have been a frightening gamble. Dick O'Mara remembers, "There were plenty of times when Dave, very embarrassed, would ask us to hold our pay check for a couple of days. And more than once, we would take up a collection among everyone to pay for a COD package when there wasn't enough in the till or the checking account to cover it." O'Mara relates one incident on which the team can now look back and laugh. He says, "A package arrived from one of the well-known parts distributors with a $65 COD bill on it. We all scrounged around in our pockets and came up with $65. When we opened the box, the only thing we found inside was a receipt for $65! Dave was long overdue on an order, and this was how the company scammed us to get their money." Remembering the bad times, Pat O'Mara recalls, "At one point we even started trying to sell stereo equipment, just trying to generate some cash flow and income."

Dave Larsen tells an amusing story—though not funny at the time—that illustrates just how close to the bone the dealership was operating. He says, "There was a post office mail drop literally right next to the night deposit box at Gravois Bank. One night I had to deposit the day's receipts on my way home. I was exhausted, and I stuck the money pouch into the mail box. It was late at night, and I called Dave at home to tell him what I had done. He really freaked out. He knew that not having that money on deposit the next morning could literally sink the company. I thought he was going to kill me." All ended well when Dave met with the post master early the next morning, retrieved the money pouch, and delivered it to the bank. But that was not the end of the story. Larsen concludes, "You can imagine what a riot it was around the shop when a few weeks later Dave made the same mistake himself. He dropped the money in the mail box! I didn't feel so dumb after that."

There have been three or four times when Dave Mungenast could have lost it all. However, this did not alter how he treated other people. Barbara Mungenast says, "Dave was always very quiet about his business problems. He never brought his troubles home from work. He didn't complain around the house and get angry with people. But there was this ashen look on his face that I learned to recognize, and when it was really bad he would sometimes say, "We need to try not to spend too much money for a while." Dave Larsen has a similar recollection: "Even when it was really bad, Dave would come to work in a good mood. He did not want to do anything that would frighten or lower the morale of his employees." Still, eventually Dave had to close the St. Charles store and lay off his good friend, Pat O'Mara. He did it with a hand-written letter that began, "I would rather take a physical beating than tell you what I must tell you now." After advising O'Mara that he would be laid off, Mungenast continued, "Believe me when I tell you how sorry I am for interrupting your career, but I am sure you know I sincerely believed the motorcycle business offered a secure future for all of us. Needless to say, I'll help in any way possible to find employment for you, although I'm sure you will have no difficulty in bettering yourself." O'Mara says, "Dave was so distraught, I actually felt guilty about getting fired and causing him pain." Even today, both Dick and Pat O'Mara remain dear friends with their former employer. Dave Larsen explains, "Dave Mungenast does not leave people behind."

With sales harder to come by for everyone in the motorcycle business, Dave was among a group of St. Louis-area dealers who formed a dealer's association in 1968. Carl and Cathy Donelson, who have been in the business since 1962 and have known Dave since his days with Bob Schultz, recall, "We had eleven dealer members, and Dave was one of our good supporters. We thought it was necessary to generate some excitement and enthusiasm for motorcycling, so our organization started promoting Tuesday night races at a track at Granite City, Illinois, just across the river. By the third or fourth year we all had a return or our investment, and I think we generated a lot of publicity for the St. Louis motorcycle scene." Carl adds, "Dealer associations are also good so dealers can get to be friends rather than fight and shout at each other." Cathy continues, "Ever since then we have had an excellent relationship with Dave. There's never been a cross word between us or bad behavior between our businesses as competitors. We like them all: Dave, Barb, and the kids."

Cooperation and involvement in organizations for the mutual benefit of peers and competitors would become a standard practice for Dave Mungenast, played out again in the formation of a Missouri Motorcycle Dealers Association in 1972, which grew rapidly to a thousand members. A sliding scale dues for dealer members based on unit sales was designed to distribute the load, enlisting small dealers for as little as $35 a year, but going up to $900 a year for dealers who sold more than 1,000 units. Dave helped devise the dues structure and served as president. At a Motorcycle Industry Council conference in Florida in

Dave and his staff celebrate the grand opening of his new Honda motorcycle dealership on Lindbergh Boulevard, 1975.

1973, industry leaders and other dealers expressed astonishment at the MMDA's rate of recruitment, and Dave was asked to give a presentation. Dave recalls, "At least 20 people asked me for copies of our dues scale, and a lot more people wrote me after I got back, asking for information."[1] Such an experience made Mungenast a believer in organized, mutual cooperation, which would play out again in the St. Louis Automobile Dealers Association where both Dave and Dave, Jr. have served as president. Eventually, the principle would lead Dave to the chairmanship of the American International Automobile Dealers Association.

[1] "Inside Dave Mungenast" by Dave Sanderson, *Cycle News East*, June 5, 1973, page 18.

Dave Mungenast and his staff at the new Honda store on Lindbergh Boulevard in 1975. Left to right: Carlo Martellaro, Chuck Van Camp, Eddie Viermann, Pat Haggarty, Greer Cavagnaro, Dave Larsen, Dave Mungenast, Carl Mungenast, and Don Levin.

Over the next four decades, Dave Mungenast would see the motorcycle business rise and fall again and again, driven by the vicissitudes of the economy. In 1975 his dealership was moved from the old storefront on Gravois to an attractive new purpose-built facility at 5935 Lindbergh Boulevard, where it remains today under the name of Dave Mungenast Motor Sports, offering not just Honda motorcycles, but the company's line of lawn and power products, as well as all-terrain vehicles. Since 2004, the business has been managed by Tim Bonagurio, a St. Louis native who learned the retail auto trade at Bianco Oldsmobile, a company that disappeared with the demise of the Oldsmobile brand. Bonagurio regarded Bianco, a family-run company, a highly ethical place to work, and his experience working under those values in part attracted him to the Mungenast businesses. He says, "There was only one person in my mind with the moral character of the Biancos, and that was Dave Mungenast."

Though there is potentially more money in automobile retail management, Bonagurio considers himself fortunate to be running Dave Mungenast Motor Sports. This is because of the nature of its customers and because it is close to Dave's heart. Bonagurio explains, "Most people don't want to buy a car. They

Dave with Eddie Viermann and Dave Larsen at a grueling event called "The Burn" in 1978. Larsen says, "The photographer wrote the year on my chest so we wouldn't forget when the picture was taken."

have to. People buy motorcycles because they really want one. They are a product of passion, and when people walk into the showroom, it is because they really want to be here. Among all the store managers, I am the lucky one because I am running with Senior's passion. This is where his roots are."[2] Charlie Keller, a 29-year veteran of American Honda who has dealt with Mungenast in both his motorcycle and automobile enterprises, sees Dave as characteristic of the very company and its founder. He says, "As large as Soichiro Honda became in the world automobile industry and other power products, he never lost his love of motorcycles. They were where his business began, and where

[2] With the emergence of David Mungenast, Jr. and his brothers Ray and Kurt as executives in the Mungenast family of businesses, Dave has become known as "Senior" by his associates and employees.

his heart remained for all of his life. Dave has followed a similar path."

Indeed, in the greater scheme of things—among the sales volume of Honda cars, Lexus, Acura, Toyota, Dodge, yachts, and the Mungenast commercial properties—the yield at the motorcycle store is barely a blip on the radar. However, it is a business that Dave will always nurture and maintain. Motorcycles are where he began, and they are where his heart remains.

CHAPTER FIVE

World-class Biker: Dave Earns His Blue Helmet

Dave starts the Baja 1000 in 1972.

Denver attorney Ted Bendelow has motor racing in his blood. His father built Meyer-Drake racing engines, he grew up around racing people, and he became a skilled and enthusiastic motorcyclist, both on and off the road. In his professional capacity he has served as legal counsel for leading national motor sports governing bodies, including the Sports Car Club of America and the American Historic Racing Motorcycle Association. Ted knows all about motor sports, but he did not know about the blue and white helmet. A few years ago, Ted was participating in Wally Dallenbach's Colorado 500 Off-Road Ride. Bendelow knew the off-road maestro Malcolm Smith, who had starred in the box office hit "On Any Sunday," and he noticed that Smith was with another man, both of whom were wearing blue helmets with two white stripes over the top. On one side of the helmet was an American flag, and the block letters "USA" were on the other. Ted says, "I had no idea what that helmet stood for, but I knew Malcolm knew what he was doing, so I tagged on behind them on the trail. They were incredible. I could not believe the grace and ease with which they attacked the difficult terrain."

Bendelow recalls, "Coming down into Silverton from Engineer's Pass, we were on a county road, going about 50 miles per hour, approaching an "S" curve. Malcolm never let off the throttle, nor did the other man. They both went into the corner sliding the back wheel of their bikes, which anyone can do. Then, without letting off the throttle, they both flipped the handlebars, full-lock in the other direction, reversing their slide as they flipped their bikes to the opposite side to complete the "S" turn, still at speed. I had never seen anyone do that before. I literally stopped my bike, I was so amazed at what I had seen and did not believe possible."

Bendelow concludes, "When I caught up with them in Silverton, they were sitting on the sidewalk with their helmets off. They obviously had been there a while. I expressed my amazement at how they negotiated the fast turn, and they actually did not remember the incident. It was so natural to them; it was just part of the ride. I was in awe. Then Malcolm introduced me to his riding buddy who also wore a blue and white helmet. It was Dave Mungenast."

Decades ago, the leading international motor sport governing bodies—the International Automobile Federation, the Federation for International Motorcycling, and others—agreed on a menu of official national colors to be used in international competition. Those chosen for the United States were blue and white. Sometimes they have appeared on automobiles or helmets as blue racing stripes on a field of white, but the more popular version is two white stripes on a field of blue. Those who wear that blue helmet are men who have represented the United States at the highest and most difficult level of international, world-class competition.

While Mungenast is skilled at all aspects of motorcycle riding, his tastes lean toward events where stamina and strategy are more important than all-out speed. His skills in this kind of competition were developed over years of riding with his friends of the Midwest Enduro Team motorcycle club. An enduro is an all-terrain event where strategy and time-keeping are paramount. Along the route are check points, and riders can lose points for arriving at a check point early or late. They are supposed to arrive on the exact minute that will insure they have maintained a consistent 24 mile-per-hour average speed over the course. Those who have not done it cannot realize how fast and hectic 24 mph can seem over rough terrain or through a tight woods section. It requires not just skill, but excellent physical conditioning and, most of all, mental discipline. Beyond these prerequisites, endurance riding requires an almost fanatical level of determination and will to finish. Since an enduro is more about finishing than winning, all of the leading enduro riders are men who earned a reputation for completing difficult events while nursing injuries that would make any normal person quit.

In 1964, the year that Dave decided to become a Honda motorcycle dealer, he gave the brand its first national championship title in American competition by winning the 24-Hour Marathon at Riverdale Speedway, near St. Louis, aboard a Honda CL72 Scrambler. Unlike an off-road enduro, in this event speed was a determining factor. An individual was required to circle the track for a 24-hour period, and the person who traveled the greatest distance was the winner. Among the class winners at Riverdale almost every year were women as well as men. Under such conditions, stamina, mental discipline, and the determination to win become far more important than out-right speed. Those who expect to run at top speed for 24 hours will likely not finish such an event. They will destroy their motorcycles or crash trying.

Mungenast was not able to enter the Riverdale Marathon in 1965, having performed the astonishing feat of both breaking his leg and winning his class at the prestigious Jack Pine Enduro in Michigan. He explains, "I was riding a little Honda S90, and here came a man down the trail, traveling the wrong way on a big British bike that was twice the weight of mine. The collision broke my leg and bent the forks of my bike back so it would barely turn. I got the guy who ran into me to start my bike, which I could not do because of my leg, and I rode on to the next check point where they took me to the hospital. Later, after returning home with my leg in a cast to the hip, I learned that I actually won my class." This is testimony to how difficult the Jack Pine can be, when a non-finisher can earn the highest score among his peers. In 1966, Dave raced at Riverdale again, winning it to become a holder of two national championship titles by the age of 22.[1]

The year that Mungenast won his second marathon championship, a California entrepreneur named Edison Dye introduced the Swedish-built Husqvarna off-road motorcycle with spectacu-

[1] Although Mungenast could not compete in the Riverdale Marathon in 1965 due to his broken leg, his friend and employee Dave Larsen won his class, giving the St. Louis Honda team three straight years of success at the event.

lar results when he brought over motocross world champion Torsten Hallman to conduct exhibitions at races and off-road events up and down the west coast. The potent Husky and Hallman's athletic riding style captured the imagination of fans and the motorcycle press, opening America to a higher level of interest in international motorcycling. The following year, St. Louis Honda began selling the Husqvarna line, and Edison Dye, upon the recommendation of John Penton, who was the Husqvarna distributor of the eastern United States, proposed that Dave compete at the International Six Day Trial, scheduled to take place later that year in Zachopane, Poland. Most Americans, including Mungenast, knew little or nothing about the ISDT. However, interest had grown after Bud Ekins and the British Triumph factory fielded America's first official team in 1964, consisting of Ekins, his brother Dave, Cliff Coleman, and actor Steve McQueen, whose star power earned attention both in the United States and Great Britain.[2]

The International Six Day Trial, commonly known among its followers as the "Six Days," is an off-road event similar to an American enduro, but it embodies significant differences in scoring, rules, and philosophy. It was conceived to be the ultimate test for man and machine in an era when most industrialized nations of Europe built motorcycles. The event was highly nationalistic, proving which nations built the best motorcycles and trained the best riders. It was an exhaustingly long event, covering up to 200 miles of difficult terrain per day for six straight days. In addition to the long days of riding, contestants were subjected to acceleration, racing, and hill climbing tests where they were measured for all-out speed, for which they earned "evaluation points." Throughout the event, a rider was not allowed to make any significant repairs to his motorcycle. Critical components on each machine were marked with seals to eliminate tampering, and other than replacing tires and drive chains, one had to just pray that his motorcycle would last the full six days. For this reason, Six Days riders had to understand how to avoid punishing their mounts under punishing conditions. Like an Enduro, there were checkpoints throughout the course, and if a rider arrived a single minute late, he would lose a "mark." To earn a gold medal, one must complete the event with a perfect score, having lost not a single minute from the prescribed schedule over nearly a thou-

[2] The story of America's first ISDT team is told in "Steve McQueen 40 Summers Ago; Hollywood Behind the Iron Curtain," 2004, Cycleman Books.

sand miles of extremely difficult riding. A rider could earn a silver medal by losing no more than 25 marks, plus evaluation points within a percentage range of his class. Finally, for just finishing the event within an hour of his key time, a rider would earn a bronze medal. Just finishing was no mean feat.[3]

Edison Dye's selection of Mungenast to ride for Husqvarna in Poland in 1967 proved a good choice, as Dave made a perfect score to earn a gold medal in his first ISDT. He found himself among the elite of American off-road riding, including Bud Ekins, Malcolm Smith, Leroy Winters, John Nelson, and John Penton. Penton, nearly ten year's Dave's senior, was on the threshold of becoming one of most important influences in the evolution of the sport. Like others of his generation, Penton learned to compete in off-road events by modifying standard, heavy motorcycles designed for the highway. The purpose-built racing motorcycle had emerged in the early 1960s for motocross, but off-road endurance riders were still working largely with modified, compromised equipment. It was Penton's vision to create a purpose-built enduro machine that could be acquired from a local dealer at a reasonable price. He began collaboration with the Austrian firm KTM to design and build such a motorcycle, and the Penton was introduced in America the following March. Mungenast, having an interest in selling the latest and best off-road motorcycles at St. Louis Honda, immediately became a Penton dealer. At that time, Pentons had 100 and 125cc engines, and Husqvarna's were 250cc or larger, so they made ideal stablemates for a dealership that wanted to offer a full range of off-road motorcycles.[4] Over the years, St. Louis Honda carried 11 different brands of motorcycles in its policy of offering the latest and the best.[5]

[3] The contest is described here in past tense, because in 1981 the International Six Days Trial was renamed the International Six Days Enduro (ISDE), along with significant rule changes. For example, in the ISDE a rider can make repairs to his motorcycle, as well as earn back marks lost on the trail. While it is still considered one of the most difficult endurance events in the world, some ISDT purists believe it has lost some standing in both prestige and difficulty from the time when Dave Mungenast and his colleagues were competing.

[4] The story of John Penton and his influence on off-road motorcycling is described in detail by this author's book, "John Penton and the Off-Road Motorcycle Revolution," published by Whitehorse Press, 2000.

[5] For some information in this chapter we are indebted to Larry Lawrence, author of Dave Mungenast's official Motorcycle Hall of Fame biography, available on the Internet at http://www.motorcyclemuseum.org/halloffame/hofbiopage.asp?id=239.

Dave, far right, with Leroy Winters, Bud Ekins, and John Penton at his first ISDT in Poland in 1967.

Dave not only became a Penton dealer, but joined the company's Six Days team for the 1968 trial, conducted in San Pellegrino, Italy. The team consisted of John Penton, his son Tom, Leroy Winters, and Dave Mungenast. Tom Penton had the best ride, with a silver medal, and all the rest finished to earn a bronze. Dave recalls, "It rained the first day of the event, and the organizers declined to go to a slower schedule, and the whole team lost its gold medals the first day." By now, Mungenast was finding it more difficult to juggle his roles as an international sportsman, a struggling business owner, and a family man. Barbara was pregnant with their third son, Kurt, and was scheduled to deliver

Dave with John Penton, Leroy Winters, and Bud Green at the Six Days in Italy in 1968.

John Penton, Leroy Winters, Tom Penton, and Dave Mungenast at the Six Days in Italy, 1968.

while Dave was away. Today he smiles and says, "Kurt decided to cooperate. He was late and arrived just after I returned home from Italy. That made things better, although Barbara was not very happy about my being away." Barbara recalls, "Dave was away so much in remote places in countries like Poland, Spain, and Italy. We did not have the kind of easy phone service we have today, and I never knew what was going on. If he was hurt, I would usually not know about it until he returned home."

Dave stayed with the Penton team for the 1969 ISDT, which took place in Garmisch-Partenkirchen, West Germany. However, an accident at the Jack Pine put his ride in jeopardy. He explains, "I crashed toward the end of the first day and dislocated my shoulder. My friend Dave Charleville took me to the hospital, and we were careful not to let John Penton know what happened because I was afraid he would replace me on the team." Faced with the necessity of toughing it out to keep his Six Days ride, Dave rode the second day of the Jack Pine, earning a third place in his class. His perseverance paid off, because the following week in Germany he earned a silver medal. Also that year, he earned a gold medal at the Berkshire International Trial, held near Pittsfield, Massachusetts. At the time, the Berkshire was the only event in the United States that followed ISDT-type international rules, and it was considered essential training for those who wanted to become better Six Days riders. During his first two seasons on the Penton team, Dave developed what would become a life-long friendship with John Penton. He would return to the Penton team once more, riding at the Isle of Man in 1971 where he would earn a gold medal.

Mungenast experienced his first failure to finish a Six Days in El Escorial, Spain in 1970, due to a disastrous crash. Falling hard on the third day, he knocked himself out, broke several ribs, and tore some ribs away from his spinal column. Two German spectators found Dave on the trail and took him to a hospital. As bad luck would have it, a brief news report mentioning the event and Dave's mishap made it into the *St. Louis Dispatch*, which is how Barbara learned about Dave's injuries. However, his failure to earn a medal in Spain did not dissuade him. In fact, he was so hooked on the ISDT, he established a personal goal to compete ten years in succession. Following his successful ride aboard a Penton at the Isle of Man in 1971, he was invited by American Honda to ride a special works XL250 in Czechoslovakia in 1972, where he experienced his second DNF (did not finish). Dave ex-

Dave at a checkpoint at a cold Six Days in Germany, 1969. Siegfried Heim photo.

plains, "A foot peg broke off and the starter gear broke. I have such faith in Honda's products, I wish they had just left well enough alone. I would rather have ridden a production motorcycle than their trick experimental works machine." By now, Kurt was two, and Barbara joined Dave at the Six Days in Czechoslovakia. Ironically, Dave's failure to finish had a positive result,

In Germany, 1969.

leaving him more time with Barb to enjoy the experience and support the team. Tom Heininger, a prominent man in the motorcycle industry at the time, recalls, "Barb is a very elegant, classy lady. We enjoyed being with her and Dave. We were all part of an American community abroad." Heininger goes on to relate that Barbara had all of her cosmetics stolen, and the other women on the tour pooled their resources to build her a new kit. Dr. Richard Meyer, physician for the American Six Days team, has similar memories: "What a spectacular couple they are. Barb was always smiling and always happy, fully supportive of Dave and the American effort. There was an intense bond between them."

Mungenast's relationship with Honda also brought him an opportunity to ride on a factory team in the Baja 1000 in November 1972, teaming up with Six Days veterans Jeff Heininger and

At the ISDT in Germany in 1969, on his way to a silver medal while riding with a dislocated shoulder. Photo Blumenthal.

Gene Cannady, Al Baker, Bill Silverthorn, and Gene Petty aboard works XL350s. The Baja 1000 was a grueling off-road race for both cars and motorcycles, running non-stop the length of the Mexican Baja peninsula. Unlike the Six Days, it is a flat-out race where teams ride around the clock at top speed over rough, desolate terrain, through stifling heat in the day and bone-chilling cold at night. It is both beautiful and brutal. While pre-riding the event to learn the terrain, the team took a break in the night to get some rest, lying down on an asphalt road to benefit from the residual heat in the pavement. Unfortunately, tarantulas and other critters know the same trick, so riders were scheduled to stand watch to chase away varmints and look for cars. Jeff Heininger remembers, "It was my turn to stand guard, and I went to sleep and was awakened by the lights of a car bearing down on us!"

For the high-speed nighttime riding in the Baja, motorcycles and cars are equipped with powerful lighting systems. Unfortunately, on the experimental Hondas the electrical systems failed, and Dave completed only two hundred miles of the race. Heininger laughs as he remembers, "The Mexicans called Dave 'Mungenez,' so that is the name he was stuck with in the Baja."

The next year was a special Six Days, being the first time the event—now nearly 50 years old—was hosted in the United States. As the Six Days grew in popularity among American off-road motorcycle enthusiasts, it became harder to qualify for a berth. The American Motorcyclist Association had created a national series of events where riders had to earn points to qualify for the Six Days. If qualifying scores were close, the AMA had final discretion to appoint or exclude a rider. Furthermore, the FIM set rider quotas for the various nations. Typically, the United States was limited to around 35 riders, and by mid-decade more than 600 were attending the qualifiers to earn their place on the team. Things had changed a great deal since the time when Edison Dye and John Penton could simply hand-pick riders for their teams. Now it required a serious commitment of time and resources to ride qualifying rounds throughout the United States to earn a place within the American contingent. Dave was stretched thin, both personally and financially. He had opened a Toyota and Volvo franchise, and was trying to get the franchise for Honda cars. Having to ride qualifying events throughout the summer while struggling to maintain businesses and provide for his family was becoming increasingly difficult.

America had become a very big motorcycle market, and every brand invested heavily in preparation for the 48th ISDT. Even those that were only marginally involved, such as BMW, had a big presence at the event. Triumph, the most successful brand in a rapidly declining British motorcycle industry, announced a big effort, fielding an official team riding specially-prepared motorcycles. As a Triumph dealer, and a man who had fond memories of his early days aboard British motorcycles, Dave applied to ride for the Triumph team. He, John Greenrose, and Ken Harvey made the cut.

Though a fierce and determined competitor, Dave Mungenast was not a man to place his own interests above the interests of the team. This was John Greenrose's first time to ride the Six Days, and he admits now that he had not developed the right temperament for the long and grueling event. He says, "People would tell me I was insane, and I took it as a compliment." Greenrose recalls, "Dave became my mentor. I was pretty wild, and during the qualifiers he would tell me, 'You shouldn't take so many chances. You have to finish to win.'" Greenrose continues, "Still, on the first day of the IDST, just about 15 miles from the start, I made a terrible mistake. There was a difficult power line section where lots of riders were bottlenecked, trying to get through a narrow place. My adrenaline was about 115% and I was chomping at the bit. I decided to ride around the whole group,

Aboard the Husqvarna in Spain, 1970.

and I stuck my Triumph in a deep hole. Dave saw what happened, and he turned off his bike, got off, and came over to help me extricate the bike and get back on course. I don't think anyone else would have done that, but this is the kind of man Dave Mungenast is."

Undoubtedly, Mungenast had sympathy for a first-timer because he had been there. About his first ISDT in Poland in 1967 he recalls, "Malcolm Smith started a position behind me that year and he told me he has never seen someone crash so much and still finish. My bike looked like it had gone through a trash

On the way to a gold medal at the Isle of Man in 1971. Photo by Jerry West.

compactor. I thought I had to go out there and ride as fast as I could. It was later I learned that you had to pace yourself so you and the machine would last for six days."[6] Dave was fortunate in Poland. Despite all the crashes, he did not totally destroy the motorcycle, and he managed a perfect score to earn a gold medal.

Greenrose was not so lucky. As a result of his rash behavior, he lost his chance for a gold medal, finishing the first day with five marks. But Dave's decision to dismount and help cost him two marks as well. Greenrose says, "That evening I felt like the

[6] *Ibid.* Motorcycle Hall of Fame; http://www.motorcyclemuseum.org/halloffame/hofbiopage.asp?id=239.

Going through technical inspection prior to the start of the ISDT in Czechoslovakia, 1972. Photo by Jerry West.

lowest person on the planet. I knew that I had damaged the standing of the team, and I was especially embarrassed that I had cost Dave Mungenast his gold medal." Dave said to Greenrose, "I'm not angry about losing those two points. This is the ISDT and stuff happens." Then he paused, thought a moment, and said with a smile, "But if I finish the event and five days from now those are the only two points I have lost, I will be pissed!" Fortunately for Greenrose, Mungenast lost another eight marks during the event, finishing with a silver medal. Greenrose concludes, "I learned from riding with Dave that year. He is aggressive, consistent, trail-smart, and very smooth. But what was even more instructive was his attitude. Nothing ever seems to fluster him. He is patient, has an even temperament, an accepting attitude, and is a delight to be around."

In the mean time, Mungenast had added Rokon to his product line at St. Louis Honda. Rokon was a small but innovative American company that had introduced a line of off-road motorcycles that featured an automatic transmission. They were also the first off-road motorcycle to use aircraft-style disc brakes. Mungenast was offered a sponsorship by Rokon to ride their

Barbara with Dave in his American team uniform at the ISDT in Dalton, Massachusetts in 1973.

bikes at the ISDT. Dave agreed, and rode Rokons at Camerino, Italy in 1974 and at the Isle of Man in 1975. In 1974, he broke his hip at a qualifying round in Barstow, California, and was unable to qualify for the American team. Rather, he entered the event under the auspices of the Canadian Motorcycle Association, and, ironically, became the only "Canadian" to finish in Italy, despite the fact that he broke his foot during the event. Borrowing a larger boot from a German rider, Dave struggled on to earn a bronze medal. Dr. Richard Meyer, the American team doctor recalls, "At night he slept with his boot on so the foot would not swell. Most people just can't imagine what a Six Days rider will tolerate to finish the event." The following year Dave again qualified for the American team, but had a disastrous time at the Isle of Man. He crashed heavily on the fourth day. He recalls, "I was very badly bruised and was worried that I might have internal injuries." He started urinating blood, which affected his morale and will to continue. Still, he struggled on, determined to finish. However, by the end of the day he was more than an hour behind his key time, which technically disqualified him from earning a finisher's medal.

The 1970s were not a good time for automobile retailers. Pollution controls had come into effect, and most manufacturers didn't yet have a clue how to build a decently-running car that

Dave at the start of the ISDT in Dalton, Massachusetts in September, 1973. Photo by Dave Arbrust.

could meet emission standards. By 1976, Dave was in conflict with his regional Toyota representative who wanted to add another dealer just down the street, and Volvo sales were really bad. Bob Sinclair, who was head of Volvo's American distributorship and would eventually become a good friend of Dave, remembers, "We were at our nadir. We built terrible cars. Owners in San Francisco could not even make it home because their clutches would burn up on the hills. Volvo wanted us to push safety, and Americans just weren't ready to hear that. All they wanted was a decent car that would run, and we weren't providing it." These were lean times at the Mungenast household, and Dave's Six Days career was coming to an end, just short of his personal goal to ride ten events.

Still, he persisted, riding qualifiers in the summer of 1976 to earn a spot on the American team. While testing a 360cc Husqvarna on Easter Sunday in preparation for a qualifier in Alabama the following week, Dave had a horrible accident, hitting at high speed a strand of barbed wire that a farmer had stretched across

Aboard the Rokon at his last ISDT at the Isle of Man in 1975.

the trail. He was not wearing his heavy competition jacket, and the wire ripped across his arm and chest, opening an artery just below his right elbow. Dave remembers, "I had a bandana around my neck, and I tied it tight around the wound. Still, all the way home, I was really worried, watching little geysers of blood pumping out of my arm. I was badly shaken, but still conscious. If I had been knocked out, I probably would have bled to death." Barbara and Dave, Jr. washed off enough blood to determine how badly Dave was injured, then rushed him to the hospital. He went on to earn four perfect scores at qualifiers that summer, but still he was not approved by the AMA to make the team. Dave says, "I was very upset at the time. I was set on completing ten events, and it was devastating to be declined my final chance. I probably could have entered the event with the Canadian team, but I decided maybe someone was telling me it was time to move on." In retrospect, he adds, "It was a changing of the guard. There were so many young riders coming up who wanted to ride the Six Days, and guys like John Penton and Malcolm Smith and I had been there for a long time. The AMA wanted to bring new blood into the American effort, and they were not wrong to want that."

Dave Mungenast's career as a world-class motorcycle competitor had come to an end. He was 42 years old and had sons who would soon be old enough to qualify for international competition. In fact, just five years later Ray began his Six Days career, competing five years in succession and finishing every year to earn three silver and two bronze medals. How Dave was able to devote so much time and energy to international competition during a decade when his businesses were struggling to survive rests in the fact that he was supported by a strong, competent, and loyal team. Barbara was a key factor in that success, capably raising the kids and keeping the family intact during the times when Dave was away. On the business side he had Dave Larsen handling the motorcycle store, Don Levin tending the automobile business, and Patty Ramsey running the office. Ramsey recalls, "When I came to work for Dave in 1973, I did not see him for the first three weeks." Three decades later, all three of these key employees, plus Dave's family, remain critical to his success. Building a strong team, learning to delegate and trust, and providing the kind of support and fair policies that would lead to employee longevity would become some of his key attributes in building a family of successful businesses.

Still, for Dave, not riding another Six Days was not the end of his opportunities to enjoy motorcycling. He worked as support crew for Ray, and still today, three decades later, he enters annual off-road events, some of which facilitate his work as a philanthropist. These include the annual Leroy Winters Memorial Six Days Reunion, Wally Dallenbach's Colorado 500 Off-Road Ride, and Malcolm Smith's Baja Ride.

The Six Days Reunion was begun by, and now named for Dave's late friend Leroy Winters, with whom he first rode at the ISDT in San Pellegrino, Italy in 1968. Dave has helped sponsor the event on three occasions, hosting it in Missouri where it has been organized by his employee Ron Ribolzi and members of the Missouri Mudders motorcycle club. The Colorado 500, hosted by former race car driver Wally Dallenbach, is in its 30th year and has generated more than $1 million in donations to the schools, communities, and people of western Colorado where the economy has been hit hard by closures in the mining industry.[7] In addition, the Colorado 500 supports the Blue Ribbon Coalition, a non-profit activist organization that promotes responsible recreation on public lands. With his Baja Ride, Malcolm Smith has supported the El Oasis Orphanage at Valle Trinidad, Mexico for more than a decade, providing water and irrigation, planting trees, buying vehicles, and expanding the facility's housing capacity nearly ten-fold.[8] Mungenast not only supports these programs financially, but rides the events every chance he gets.

Although these are all non-competitive, recreational events, because of the people involved—including Six Days veterans and American national champions—they can include a high degree of difficulty and considerable danger. Three-times national motocross champion Kent Howerton was riding with Mungenast at the Colorado 500 in 1984 when Dave experienced a horrendous crash that earned him the dubious honor of "worst crash of the year." Howerton recalls, "We were going up a rocky jeep road at about 35 miles per hour when Dave hit a big rock that flipped the motorcycle and catapulted him right over the handlebars. We were in big, nasty, sharp shale rocks, and it was the worst crash I have ever seen that someone walked away from. Fortunately,

[7] More information about the charitable aspects of the Colorado 500 is available on the Internet at http://www.colorado500.org/history_main.htm.

[8] More information about Malcolm Smith's Baja charity ride is available on the Internet at http://malcolmsmithrides.com/about.php.

Dave didn't have a scratch." Part of Dave's ability to continue demanding riding and survive such crashes is his physical conditioning, which he has always maintained through exercise and good diet. His friend Malcolm Smith says, "Dave is amazing. At 72, he's got the physical condition of a good 50-year-old."[9]

When he rides, Dave still wears his blue helmet with pride. He has earned the right to do so.

[9] Like Dave Mungenast, both Kent Howerton and Malcolm Smith are members of the Motorcycle Hall of Fame. Howerton's official Hall of Fame biography can be found on the Internet at http://www.motorcyclemuseum.org/halloffame/hofbiopage.asp?id=200. Smith's can be found at http://www.motorcyclemuseum.org/halloffame/hofbiopage.asp?id=91.

CHAPTER SIX

Movie Stars and Fast Company:

Dave Goes to Hollywood

When Dave Mungenast failed to make the American Six Days team in 1976, he was devastated. The door was forever closed on his ambition to ride the event ten times. However, in retrospect, Dave has said, "When one door closes, another may open, and had I been riding in Austria that year, I would not have been here to answer that phone call from Stan Barrett." Stan Barrett and Dave became friends while the Mungenast family lived at Lake Montowese, and Dave has always regarded Stan a special person. He says, "Stan is a very talented man. He has remarkable reflexes and physical ability, a quick wit, a fertile imagination, and a lot of courage."

Barrett, nine years younger than Dave, took those attributes to Hollywood in the mid-60s, where he entered the motion picture industry as a stunt man. Over time he moved up through the ranks, becoming a stunt coordinator, an assistant director, an actor, and a producer. He is still active, and since 1966 has been involved in over 75 motion picture projects. Barrett became closely associated with director and producer Hal Needham—who also had relatives in St. Louis—and during the 1980s drove in nineteen NASCAR races in the Skoal Bandit stock car, owned by Needham and Burt Reynolds. Today, his son Stanton is a NASCAR driver. Barrett's phone call to Dave Mungenast in the autumn of 1976 opened the door to a decade of excitement, danger, speed, and involvement with movie stars that would indirectly prove beneficial to Dave's business career.

Dave readily accepted Stan's invitation to try his hand at stunt work in the movies. After all, it was an opportunity to ride motorcycles—albeit dangerously—and be well paid for it. The call came when Barrett was working as stunt coordinator on the production of "Airport 77." In this movie, art thieves hijack a 747. Flying low over the ocean to avoid radar detection, they hit a fog bank and crash somewhere in the Bermuda Triangle. The 747 sinks 100 feet to the bottom intact with the passengers still alive, but it is a race against time to effect a rescue as water begins to inundate the plane. Jack Lemmon is the pilot, Captain Don Gallagher. Christopher Lee is Martin Wallace. Other stars included Darren McGavin, George Kennedy, Brenda Vaccaro, Lee Grant, Joseph Cotton, and Olivia de Havilland.

The script called for Lemmon and Christopher Lee to go into the leaking cargo hold of the aircraft. There they must open a cargo door to gain access out of the airplane, knowing that tons of ocean water will crash in on them as soon as the door is released. The character Wallace (Christopher Lee) will die by drowning in the attempt, and filming required a stunt that was as dangerous in reality as it was in simulation. Knowing of Mungenast's underwater demolition training in the Army Special Forces, Barrett recruited Dave for the job. Doubling for Christopher Lee, Dave pulled the door open and was blasted across the hull of the aircraft and into a cargo net. As the hold began to fill with water, Dave was required to stay submerged for a long period while filming continued, creating the illusion that Wallace had drowned. Dave recalls, "The set was built on a tank with 14,000 gallons of water behind the door. When I opened it, it was like being hit in the face and chest with a fire hose." Stunt men call their stunts "gags," but Dave's first motion picture gag as a professional stunt man was no laughing matter.

Next came "The End," a black comedy starring and directed by Burt Reynolds. Reynolds plays Sonny Lawson, a terminally ill man who ends up in a psych ward following a botched suicide attempt. There he meets Dom DeLuise, a demented schizophrenic who is happy to help Sonny finish the job, even after Sonny has decided he wants to live the time he has left. Other stars in the film included Sally Field, Carl Reiner, Myrna Loy, and Kristy McNichol. Reynolds and the manic DeLuise achieved a comic chemistry in this move that would be played

Dave with Burt Reynolds in "The End."

out again and again over the next decade in a series of successful slapstick comedies. In this movie, Mungenast played a motorcycle cop who was run off the road, into a hedge, and fell back, getting up to shake his fist at Burt Reynolds.

There was also a stunt in "The End" that did not make it into the movie, and it was one of Dave's favorites. The script called for a car carrier driver to deliver a Volvo to a woman. The Volvo is the only remaining car on the carrier, and it is parked far forward, just over the cab of the truck. The woman is concerned about her car, and admonishes the driver to be careful. He assures her the he has done this many times, and never put a scratch on a customer's car. When he climbs up into the Volvo to back in down the ramps, an approaching automobile is driven off the road by a reckless Burt Reynolds who rounds a turn in a Jaguar on the wrong side of the street. The motorist, played by Stan Barrett, roars up the ramps of the car carrier, and knocks the Volvo off the front of the truck and into the street.

Dave recalls, "Everyone was really worried about this stunt. No one had done it before, and they wanted to install a special seat in the Volvo with a five-point racing harness. I said, 'No, let's make this look as realistic as possible. I'll do it with just the standard seat belt.'" Dave continues, "I helped design the stunt. I belted myself in the Volvo and started the engine. I held one foot on the brake and loaded the accelerator so the engine was racing as fast as possible without making the car move forward. Barrett drove up the ramps and barely touched me, but it looked faster and more violent than it was because at that moment I let off the brake and gave it the gas. The Volvo shot off the front of the car carrier. It made a nice trajectory and landed on its nose, and the hood flew open. Then it crashed down in the rear, causing the trunk lid to fly up." He concludes, "Immediately after the shot the nurse came running over and said, 'Are you okay? You were flopping around in there like a rag doll.' I was fine, and everyone was hysterical. They thought it was a huge success, but, unfortunately, it was kind of an afterthought in the script and did not make it into the final cut."

Later that year, Dave was invited back to work on "Hooper," another Hal Needham-directed movie starring Burt Reynolds. Sonny Hooper (Reynolds) is a leading Hollywood stuntman who is at the top of his game, but feeling the aches and pains of a long career of abusing his body. In possibly the most memorable line from the movie, he says, "I'm gonna find the guy who invented Xylocaine and kiss his ass on Hollywood and Vine." Hooper's alpha male status is challenged by young, up-and-coming stuntman Ski Chinski, played by Jan-Michael Vincent, but through sharing the danger of their business, they bond and become fast friends by the end of the story. Sally Field is back as Gwen Doyle, Hooper's significant other, who is the daughter of Jocko Doyle, a grizzled stuntman old-timer who understands the doubt and pain Hooper is hiding under his macho bravado. Other stars in the film included Adam West and Terry Bradshaw.

Robert Klein plays demanding and arrogant director Roger Deal, a character rumored to be modeled after Peter Bogdanovich. Not surprisingly, in a movie about stuntmen, the plot was contrived to depict as many stunts as possible. The movie

Dave, playing a motorcycle cop, gives a ticket to Hooper, played by Burt Reynolds. Moments later Dave is yanked off his speeding motorcycle.

within a movie format gave director Needham many opportunities to reveal some of the illusions and safety secrets behind the craft of the Hollywood stuntman. The story ends with the stunt of the century, described in the film as "Damnation Alley," where Hooper and Ski race their car through a protracted scene, surrounded by explosions and collapsing buildings, only to see the bridge to their escape collapse, requiring them to jump their car across a long, deep chasm.

In "Hooper," Mungenast got a speaking part while repeating his role as a motorcycle cop. In this case, he chases down Hooper, who is nonchalantly speeding down the highway backwards, on his way to the Palomino Club to knock back some beers with his stuntman buddies. The cop pulls him over and engages in banter with the wiseacre Hooper as he writes him a ticket. Distracted by the conversation, the cop does not realize that Hooper's madcap buddies have sneaked up and attached a steel cable to his belt. The other end of the cable is attached to a telephone pole, and as the cop speeds off, he is yanked off the back of his motorcycle, which careens and crashes in the center of the highway. Dave explains that this stunt is officially known as a "jerk off," and uses a shock-absorbing device that makes it less violent and dangerous than it appears on screen. Mungenast also

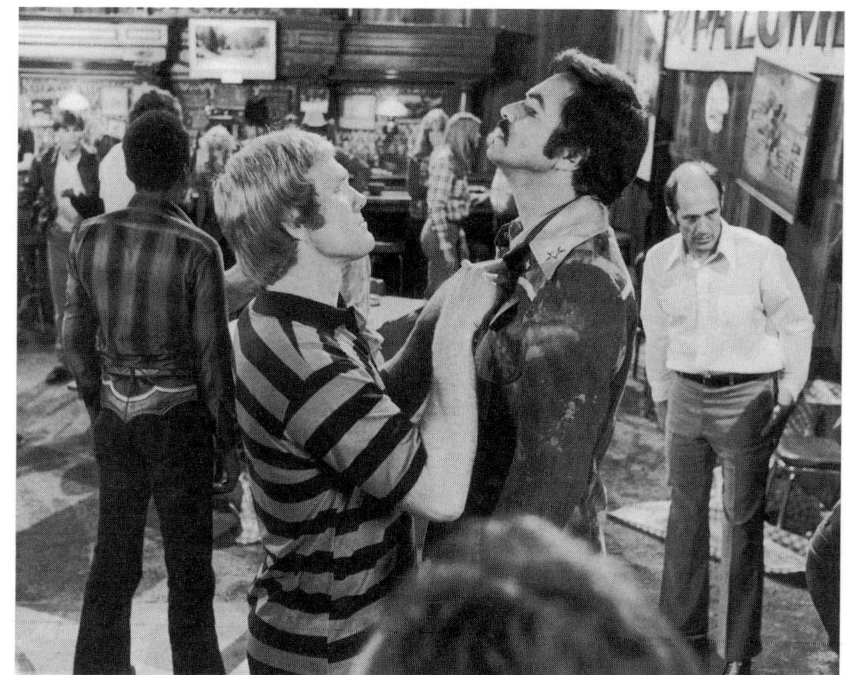

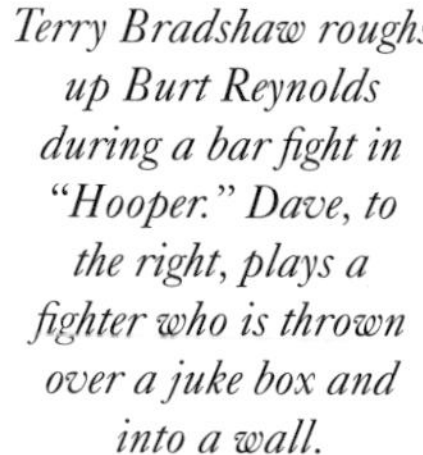

Terry Bradshaw roughs up Burt Reynolds during a bar fight in "Hooper." Dave, to the right, plays a fighter who is thrown over a juke box and into a wall.

did some motorcycle crashes and is beaten up in a wreck-the-whole-room bar fight at the Palomino Club. Dave recalls, "There was a scene where one of the bar fighters—actually a pro football player friend of Terry Bradshaw—picks me up and tosses me over a jukebox and into the wall. We had to shoot that scene about five times. It beat me up worse than any motorcycle stunt I ever did." After the day's shooting, Reynolds introduced Dave to his favorite massage parlor. Dave adds, "I was still almost too sore to move when I flew back home to St. Louis.

In "Hooper," we learn that stuntmen are a tight-knit community. They work together, play together, drink together, and fight together, always acting out their mutual respect and professional camaraderie through cruel jokes and oneupmanship. Dave explains, "That's really what it's like. They are a very closed fraternity, almost a cult. They are always gossiping and back-biting among themselves, but they will defend each other to the death against the outside world. I was not a member of their fraternity, and I was kind of odd man out. I would fly in, do my stunts, collect my pay, then fly back to St. Louis. I'm sure they were all saying, 'Who is that guy?' "

Director Needham, Reynolds, and DeLuise teamed up again in 1981 to create the legendary "Cannonball Run," written by

Brock Yates, based on transcontinental outlaw racing that allegedly really happened. With fast cars, big-breasted women, frustrated cops, and the requirement of getting from one coast to the other as quickly as possible, practically no plot was required. Rather, the film was carried by stunts and star power, including Roger Moore, Farrah Fawcett, Dean Martin, Sammy Davis, Jr., Jack Elam, Adrienne Barbeau, Terry Bradshaw, Jamie Farr, Peter Fonda, Bert Convy, and Jackie Chan, appearing in his first movie in America. Mungenast's stunts in "Cannonball Run" included motorcycle crashes and participation in the obligatory biker brawl with Peter Fonda. Still, he says, the most harrowing stunt was a scene where Jackie Chan knocks out two bikers simultaneously. Dave explains, "Chan walks between us, and the script called for him to leap high in the air, doing the splits in mid-air and kicking us both in the face. My part called for me to just stand there and probably get my head kicked in. But he was incredible. He could leap and kick out, and his foot would pass within less than an inch of my nose. His accuracy was unbelievable."

He didn't plan it this way, but back in St. Louis Dave benefited from his stunt work in Hollywood. By this time his business had finally begun to take off. In 1974 he acquired a Honda car franchise, the following year his motorcycle dealership expanded from the small Gravois store front to a purpose-built facility on Lindbergh, and by 1978 he was heralded in the *St. Louis Post-Dispatch* as the city's leading Honda dealer. This was a time when automobile dealers still relied heavily on local television to get their message across, and there was no limit to the stunts some would perform to get the viewer's attention. Benchmark among these notorious commercials was California's Cal Worthington who would ride in on a hippopotamus, announcing, "I'll eat a bug! I'll kiss a pig! I'll do anything to sell you a car!" Dave Mungenast also created his own commercials, but his stunts were real, seen in clips from the box office hits where he had performed death-defying feats. He recalls, "It was very good for business. I earned tremendous recognition in the St. Louis market from my stunt work. Stories about me began to appear in the local newspapers."

Dave's work on the big screen also earned him exposure on the small screen. In 1981, Hal Needham was asked to appear on "To Tell the Truth." He was not available, and recommended that Mungenast take his place. "To Tell the Truth" was a popular television show where a panel of celebrities tried to identify who was telling the truth among three contestants, two of whom were imposters. In this case, the person the panel was trying to identify was "the Cactus Cop," a guy whose job it was to run down people who stole endangered Saguaro Cactus from the southwestern American deserts. Dave says, "I flew to New York and pretended to be the Cactus Cop. The panel identified me as an imposter, in part because the real guy was about 20 years older than I was at the time." Still, Dave got the opportunity to identify himself as a St. Louis automobile dealer on national television. He recalls, "It got me a lot of recognition and exposure in St. Louis." When Dave next returned to Beffa's Restaurant, his usual lunch hangout, there was a potted cactus waiting for him. Dave says, "Barb still has it."

Recognition of Dave Mungenast as a man of action who worked with Burt Reynolds, Paul Newman, Peter Fonda, and other members of Hollywood's rich and famous led to a strategic repositioning of his businesses that helped shape their style and future. Dave is a humble person, and he had always shied away from putting his name out front. Mel Breckenridge, his advertising consultant, thought this a missed opportunity. He explained to Dave that people did not talk to their friends about buying a vehicle from St. Louis Honda. They talked about buying it from Dave Mungenast, a man who had earned a reputation for fair dealing and extraordinary customer service. As much as Dave might dislike it, his success was based on his name, personality and reputation, and Breckenridge knew that "Dave Mungenast" was becoming a brand in the St. Louis market. He persuaded Dave to rename his businesses "Dave Mungenast St. Louis Honda." In 1947, Soichiro Honda—one of Dave's heroes—said, "Engineering without personality doesn't have much value." This may be true in sales and marketing as well. Breckenridge knew and Dave began to understand that the value of his businesses rested in the personality that customers associated with the name "Dave Mungenast."

In 1984, Dave Mungenast the stunt man got a change of pace, working on "Harry and Son," directed by Paul Newman and staring Newman, Robby Benson, Ellen Barkin, Ossie Davis, Morgan Freeman, and Joanne Woodward. Unlike the Burt Reynolds comedies, this was a serious drama that relied on character rather than action. Harry Keach (Newman) is a gruff, inarticulate wrecking ball operator who has a hard time admitting that is losing his edge as well as his eyesight. Dave plays Max, a laborer who Keach nearly kills with his a wrecking ball. Later

On the set with Paul Newman in "Harry and Son."

that year, Mungenast performed in "Welcome to Paradise," a pilot shot in New Zealand for a television series that was never released. In this film Dave, Gary Davis, and Dennis Scott jumped motorcycles 120 feet through the air off of a pier, and plunged 45 feet into the ocean. It was a dangerous stunt that earned them nomination for Stuntmen of the Year, the equivalent of an Oscar in the stuntman profession. Later, Dave told *St. Louis Globe-Democrat* columnist John Auble, "It was absolutely the most terrifying time of my life. I'll tell you one thing, I'll never try anything that dangerous again."[1] Dave was 49 years old at the time, his business was beginning to take off, and the horrific gag down under might have been a signal that it was time for Dave to end the stuntman chapter of his life. His final film was "Stormin' Home," a 1985 Jerry Jameson directed movie about an aging motocross racer. In this movie, Dave got the opportunity to perform stunts with Kent Howerton, one of America's top motocross champions. With amusement, Howerton recalls, "I got to crash Dave off the race track on his 50th birthday!" The other riders, most of whom were in their twenties, gained a great respect for Mungenast. Howerton explains, "Dave was fast, and not just on the race track. He challenged the rest of us young riders to

[1] "In Our Town" by John Auble, *St. Louis Globe-Democrat*, April 14–15, 1984.

Dave, playing Max, a construction worker who is almost hit by a wrecking ball operated by Harry, played by Paul Newman.

race to the mess tent, and he beat most, including me!" Howerton adds, "One of the best times I ever had was on that set, working with Dave and Stan Barrett. They were great guys. Dave is an enjoyable person to be around. He is upbeat and always has great stories to tell."

Dave's stunt career and friendship with Stan Barrett led to yet another once-in-a-lifetime opportunity during this remarkable period in Dave's life. In the mid-1970s, Hal Needham teamed up with rocket engineer Bill Fredrick to build a wheeled vehicle that could surpass the speed of sound. In 1976, Needham piloted the Fredrick-designed SMI Motivator to a speed of more than 600 miles per hour at the Alvord Desert in Oregon. In December 1979, they brought to Edwards Air Force Base in Southern California the Budweiser Rocket, a three-wheeled, 5,000 pound vehicle, just under 40 feet in length, packing a 48,000 horsepower engine capable of moving the machine from a standing start to 140 miles per hour in the first second, and beyond 400 miles per hour in three seconds. Stan Barrett was chosen to drive the machine, and Dave Mungenast was part of the crew, driving an emergency vehicle. Barrett later described the experience:

At Edwards Air Force Base in December 1979. Dave, left, talks with rocket car pilot Stan Barrett, right, during preparation for the sound barrier assault.

> What a sobering moment as I looked before me at the dry lake bed where so many committed men had lost their lives. . . . I can remember very vividly as I looked out the windshield down the fuselage of the rocket and the vastness in front of me as the crew busied themselves with the task of readying the rocket for its sternest test. . . . Neither I, nor anyone else knew what might happen. God alone knew what course this battle was to take from the beginning and what the outcome would be.[2]

The outcome was spectacular. On December 19, 1979, the monitoring system created by Frederick determined that the Budweiser Rocket achieved a terminal speed of 739.666 miles per hour. Although the results have remained controversial due to the measuring methodology,[3] it is believed by experts, includ-

[2] From the foreword to "The Land Speed Record" by J.R. Holthusen, Haynes Publishing.

[3] Traditionally, land speed records are established by radar or photoelectric timing devices operated by impartial experts that measure speed over a measured distance, and certified by an independent governing authority with longstanding experience. The speed of the Budweiser Rocket was calculated by measuring rate of acceleration and terminal velocity with equipment operated by the owners of the vehicle. The attempt was supervised by the International Hot Rod Association, an organization with no experience in measuring or certifying land speed records. Chuck Yeager, the first

ing Chuck Yeager, that the machine exceeded the speed of sound, and there is no doubt that Stan Barrett became the fastest man on Earth.

Dave Mungenast has in his office a model of the Budweiser Rocket and a photograph of himself, squeezed into Barrett's fire proof driving suit, standing by the vehicle. He says, "Stan is considerably smaller than I am. It was hard enough to get into his suit. There is no way I could fit into the cockpit of the car." He also keeps with great pride a handwritten note from Barrett that says, "Brother Dave, What can I say? You have shared and supported me in such a large part of my life. You have been more than a brother and more than a friend. We shared in this challenge and once again did it together. You are a testament to true friendship."

Fast company, indeed!

---

man to break the speed of sound in an aircraft, offered his opinion in writing that the Budweiser Rocket had broken the sound barrier. A more detailed commentary on the controversial nature of the claim can be found on the Internet at http://www.roadsters.com/bud/.

CHAPTER SEVEN

Motorcycles, Automobiles, Marina, and More: The Family of Businesses Grows

Dave Mungenast had owned his motorcycle dealership for a little over a year when he acquired a Toyota franchise in the summer of 1966, obtaining a $10,000 line of credit and paying $350 a month to rent a 6,000 square foot facility at 5625 Gravois, just up the street from his motorcycle store. There was no car lot, and the showroom was large enough to hold only a couple of cars. It was an inauspicious beginning, and Dave was to learn the hard lesson that selling Japanese cars was not like selling motorcycles. For the most part, motorcyclists are adventuresome people looking for thrills and excitement, buying motorcycles to fulfill an emotional need. People buy automobiles from a totally different frame of mind, looking for comfort, convenience, reliability, and possibly status. The introduction and surprising success of Volkswagen in the American market had benefited from the myth of superior German engineering. Despite what the Japanese had proven with their motorcycles, in the mid-1960s Americans still had an attitude that Japanese automobiles were junk. The urban legend prevailed that they were actually made from recycled beer cans. It did not help that the early imports had a rust problem, causing the bodies of some Toyotas to literally rust away before the cars experienced any kind of mechanical problems.

Don Levin, who met Dave when he was at Bob Schultz's, worked at a Volkswagen dealership at the time, and says, "Most

Dave has his first meeting with Soichiro Honda in Japan, 1965.

of the guys who got into the import car business had a vision, but no money. That was the case with Dave, and beyond a thin line of credit, Dave had nothing to keep the business going. By Christmas they had sold only eight or nine cars, and had some trade-ins that weren't moving. They were in a negative cash position that was getting worse when Dave asked me to lunch to seek my advice." Don continues, "We had white-bread hamburgers, and I told him I thought he should just close down the company and start over, which is essentially what he did." Dave pursued Don to help him restart the business, and on February 15, 1967, Levin went to work for Dave. He recalls, "I got paid $300 a month, plus an imaginary commission." Levin concludes, "Little by little we began to sell a few cars, but we were doing pretty well in the service department, attracting a lot of repair work. When Toyota set up another dealer about a mile and a half away, we moved the store to Lindbergh Avenue." It did not help

Dave on the Bullet Train in Japan during his first Honda motorcycle dealer's tour in 1965.

Dave's first automobile dealership on Gravois Road.

Dave's cash flow situation that by this time his motorcycle sales were in decline due to the Vietnam War.

Mungenast added Volvo to his product line in 1971. Quality of the Swedish brand was at a low point, and Dave's policy to always try to make good for his customers consumed much of his Volvo profits in keeping the cars running. Don Levin recalls,

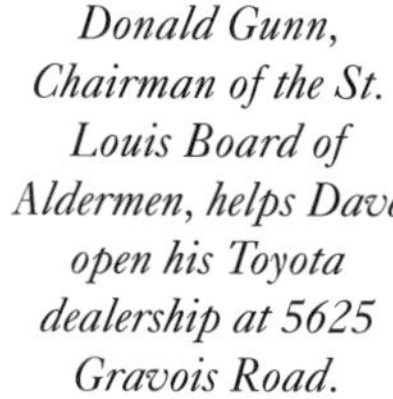

Donald Gunn, Chairman of the St. Louis Board of Aldermen, helps Dave open his Toyota dealership at 5625 Gravois Road.

"They were having labor problems at the factory in Sweden, and many of the cars arrived semi-assembled." Furthermore, problems continued with Toyota. Regional managers had a lot of autonomy and power, especially in the early days of the Japanese companies, and some of them chose to motivate sales and growth through constant threats, intimidation, and internal competition, as evidenced by the decision to install another dealer close to Dave's Gravois location. By the end of the decade, Dave had enough. In 1977 he discontinued Volvo, and in 1979 he sold his Toyota franchise. Toyota was booming in America. Over the decade, sales had doubled each year, but for the moment, Dave decided he would not go along for the ride. In retrospect, giving up his position with Toyota is a decision he would regret, stating, "It probably set me back five years in my development as an automobile dealer." Still, through his difficult early years in the automobile business, Mungenast came away with at least one powerful asset, and that was Don Levin. Levin stuck with him and remains today, and has been Dave's "start-up guy" in each new dealership he has added to his family of businesses over the past three decades. Levin declares that it was how Dave does business that caused him to stay. He states, "Dave has a charisma that makes you very willing to do things for him that you might not even want to do for yourself. He is a relationship guy who always

Dave and Barbara in Japan, 1971.

tries to treat people the way they want to be treated." Levin adds, "He made it awful easy for me not to want to go work for anyone else."

Later, through his Lexus dealership, Dave Mungenast would develop a productive relationship high up in the Toyota corporate structure where veteran executives confessed to him that they regretted and were dismayed by his decision to drop Toyota. But Dave had gotten sick of how he was treated by the regional manager, and his unhappiness may have been fueled by the fact that by the mid-1970s he had good experience with a better business model. Through his motorcycle dealership, Dave had fallen in love with Honda. He respected the product and the company, and had met and had a great admiration for Soichiro Honda on a personal level. As soon as it became evident that Honda would enter the automobile business in America, Dave was eager to become a dealer, opening on Lindbergh Road in 1974.

Honda launched its automobile business in America by selling cars only in California, Oregon, and Washington in 1970.

Dave is named a Time Magazine Quality Dealer in 1971.

The new Lindbergh Boulevard Honda car dealership, opened in 1974.

Based on that market test, Honda began to seek dealers throughout the United States in 1971. Charlie Keller, who has been in both the motorcycle and car divisions of American Honda, explains. "The early automobile line consisted of little N600 and Z600 models, which were small and had motorcycle-based engines. In 1971, the energy crisis was still a few years away, and most people didn't want little cars. Japanese products still had an

Dave and Barbara with Soichiro Honda in 1976.

image problem, and a lot of people made fun of our little Honda cars. We had a very successful motorcycle business by then, and a strong national dealer network, but we discovered that most of our dealers simply did not have the vision to take on an automobile line. Dave did." Keller continues, "I had heard about Dave before I met him. He was well known throughout American Honda for everything he had accomplished."

Tom Elliott, who was responsible for expansion in the Midwest and Northeastern states, and later became American Honda's Executive Vice President of Automobile Operations, says, "My job was to visit key markets, such as St. Louis. Of course, we knew Dave as a motorcycle dealer, but we also had identified him as a prime prospect as an automobile dealer because he had already taken on Toyota." Elliott recalls, "I first visited Dave in 1971 and found him to be exactly the kind of guy we would want to represent our product. My job of expanding Honda's automobile dealer network would have been easy if I just could have cloned Dave." Elliott's feelings seem well justified, since Dave Mungenast's St. Louis Honda has become Missouri's leading sales volume dealership, consistently earning first place in the St. Louis market and winning Honda's prestigious President's Award every year since 1998. To make room for his motorcycle dealership, which moved to a new building adjacent to the Honda automobile store in 1975, and a separate pre-owned Honda business, Dave began to buy and consolidate commercially-zoned residential property on Lindbergh. Begun by necessity for his transportation businesses, over time commercial real estate would become a separate and major segment of the Mungenast family of businesses as Dave would buy and sell, little by little parlaying his limited assets into ever larger holdings. Ron Huch, Dave's good friend from the days of their Dirty Dozen motorcycle gang who went on to build a successful career in investment banking, mergers and acquisitions, and as a turnaround expert for distressed companies, would say many years later, "The thing important about Dave is that he can grow a business off of retained earnings. It is a very extraordinary person who can do that."

Success with Honda led Dave to again step up to an opportunity when the company launched Acura, its luxury brand, in 1986. Honda and the other Japanese manufacturers had long since overcome their image problems regarding quality, and Honda became so confident in the American market that it opened a major manufacturing facility in the United States in 1981. Honda had built its American market on good quality for a low price, but Hondas had gradually grown in size, features, and price in pursuit of American buyers who had previously preferred full-size domestic automobiles. To keep its Honda brand within a moderate price range, but avoid sending its aging and more affluent customers away to German and American luxury cars, Honda became the first Japanese manufacturer to risk launching a prestige brand, a move it had been researching and anticipating since the mid-1970s. For its launch of Acura, only 50 Honda dealers were chosen throughout the nation, and only Dave Mungenast was selected for the St. Louis market.

Dave Mungenast, now well-known throughout St. Louis both for his movie exploits and his good customer service, gave Acura a dealership appropriate to its ambitious plan to establish a reputation for high quality. Dave and Honda had been researching a location for over a year, choosing five acres at 13720 Manchester Road in the growing West County. A 22,000 square foot, $2.5 million building was constructed, projecting a high-tech image featuring an interior of gleaming aluminum, mirrored

Formica, natural oak, and red highlights. With the Mungenasts, Acura got a bonus, and that was Barbara, who took responsibility for external color selection and interior design. Her creation was so successful that Acura used photographs of the dealership in its image-building brochures. It was also featured on the cover of the *St. Louis Post-Dispatch* magazine section.[1] Since its opening, the Acura dealership has been expanded and remodeled, with an increase of 11 to 19 service bays. While many dealers treat sales and service as separate profit centers with little communication between the two, Dave has always believed that good service benefits the showroom through repeat sales and referrals by satisfied customers. St. Louis Acura has won the brand's coveted Precision Team Award thirteen times.

In addition to Dave, Barbara was not the only member of the Mungenast household making a contribution to the growing family of businesses. By this time Dave, Jr. was general manager at St. Louis Honda, Ray was attending the National Automobile Dealer Association Academy in training to follow his older brother into management, and Kurt was helping part-time in the Honda parts department when not in school.

A year after he opened his Acura dealership, Dave Mungenast got an opportunity to return to the Toyota brand, acquiring a Toyota/Dodge dealership just across the river from St. Louis in Alton, Illinois. Applying the policies developed at his other dealerships, Dave has transformed this business, earning Dodge Five Star Certification and the Toyota President's Award four times. Kurt Mungenast, having finished his obligation in the military, has returned to rejoin the family business, and is working at the Alton store. Dave acquired the business from a dealer who had promoted himself as "Big-hearted Bob," a guy who was going to give you a good deal just because he was such a big-hearted guy. Big-hearted Bob starred in his own television commercials, wearing a specially-made shirt with a big red heart on the front that pulsated conspicuously while he made his pitch. Dave reports that after the deal was closed, Big-hearted Bob said, "Hey, I've got something that you need for your TV commercials, and you can continue the tradition as Big-hearted Dave." Wherewith, Bob tried to sell Dave his throbbing heart shirt for $5,000! Dave smiles and says, "I had to decline. It just wasn't my style." Then

[1] "Introducing St. Louis Acura: Precision Crafted Automobiles," *St. Louis Post-Dispatch*, September 7, 1986.

One of America's first Acura dealerships, opened on Manchester Road in 1986.

Dave in a photograph for a 1986 St. Louis Post-Dispatch cover story on the opening of the Acura dealership.

The Toyota dealership in Alton, Illinois, acquired it 1987.

he adds, "I guess he wasn't so big-hearted after all, since he wouldn't even give me the shirt off his back."

Toyota was not far behind Honda in taking aim on the luxury market. The brand had built near-luxury models in the Crown and the Cressida, but their sales paled in comparison to the huge success of Corollas and Camrys. Toyota found itself with exactly the same problem as Honda. Though known for quality, its brand image was not associated with luxury automobiles. Toyota made a huge commitment to solving this problem in the early 1980s, assigning nearly 3,000 engineers, technicians, and designers to the development of the Lexus, a car based on closer machining tolerances and higher manufacturing standards than any in history. By 1985 the company was conducting market research in the United States, and, taking dead aim at Mercedes, Toyota had prototypes in testing on the roads in America and Germany by 1986. A design was approved in 1987, and before the end of the decade Lexus hit the market with an automobile with greater luxury and reliability, but a lower price than Mercedes-Benz.

As with its Acura store, the company has paid careful attention to creating a sales and service environment compatible with the upscale clientele that gravitate to a luxury brand like Lexus. When one walks into the subdued lighting of the showroom, surrounded by dark marble and smoked glass, he or she will be greeted by a woman in a skirt and blazer, just as one might be greeted in a fine restaurant. No salesmen hover or rush forward to attack the customer. If the client is interested in looking at new or pre-owned cars, a salesperson will be assigned and introduced by the hostess. If service is required, the client will be guided to the leather couches of a well-appointed service waiting room, and a service representative will be brought in. Not surprisingly, Dave has again turned to his own family for talent, as on many days the Lexus showroom greeter is Virginia Mungenast, his sister-in-law and widow of his late brother Tom. Virginia explains, "We refer to our buyers as 'clients,' not 'customers,' because we think of them as people whom we intend to serve for many years to come. We maintain a respectful relationship with our clients by using a system that keeps salespersons from having to compete among themselves. Rather, they are assigned to customers in a rotation that is fair to everyone involved. We want our clients to leave feeling they have been served, not sold." With similar attention to detail in all departments, there is little wonder that Dave Mungenast's Lexus of St. Louis has earned the Elite of Lexus Award 11 times.

By the late 1980s, the Mungenast family of businesses was running well enough that Dave could return to his first love—motorcycles—and a little nostalgic self-indulgence. In the 35 years since he had gone into business on the eve of the post-war motorcycle sales boom, a lot had changed for both Dave and his customers. Like Dave, the Baby Boomers who fueled mid-60s motorcycle sales had gone to college, gotten married, started businesses, and raised families. Many now had time and money, and some were returning to the happy days of their youth, acquiring and restoring motorcycles from that era and creating a market for antique motorcycles and memorabilia. Dave was no exception, and over the years had built up a collection of old motorcycles. Noting the trend, in 1988 he created a small company with a British motorcycle expert named Brian Slark. Named Classic Motorcycles, the business was intended to acquire, restore and resell collectibles. It didn't work out as planned when Dave and Brian discovered most people were not willing to pay a price that would justify the time and money that went into a restoration. Slark moved on to work at the celebrated George Barber collection in Birmingham, Alabama, and Classic Motorcycles languished for the next decade.

In the meantime, the old neighborhood on Gravois Road had gone through changes too. The neighborhood had declined and

Dave Mungenast's St. Louis Lexus dealership, opened in 1989.

many storefronts were abandoned. But after the breakup of Yugoslavia, industrious Bosnian emigrants had begun to move into South City, and the neighborhood was making a comeback. With so many fond memories connected to the neighborhood, Dave got involved, renovating the old Toyota store as a new home for Classic Motorcycles, reorganized as a limited liability company for the purpose of opening a museum to display Dave's collection. Originally, it was a former motorcycle dealership employee named Becky Lewis who approached Dave with the idea of creating a museum/classic bike dealership, open to the public, to house and display his personal collection. At first Dave was skeptical, and asked her to submit a business plan. He says, "I thought that was the last I would hear of it, but she returned with a fleshed-out plan that made sense." In the process of developing the plan, Dave was reminded again how important it is to treat customers the way they want to be treated. One of the aldermen who had the power to approve or disapprove Dave's plans to renovate the old building turned out to be one of his early motorcycle customers. Dave said, "He became very enthusiastic and supportive of what we wanted to do. It did not hurt that he had good memories of buying a motorcycle from us years ago. You just never know when your past is going to come back around and affect your future." Officially opened in 2000, Classic Motorcycles LLC is now managed by Dave Larsen with the assistance of motorcycle restorer Dave Burst. Larsen seems pleased to have come full circle, tending the very motorcycles he helped assemble and sell on Gravois Road forty years ago. Dave Mungenast's Classic Motorcycles museum is free to the public, and often serves as a nostalgic setting for special motorcycle-related events.[2]

With four automobile dealerships and affiliated pre-owned sales operations, the Mungenast family of businesses has faced a growing demand for auto body work in its desire to provide full service to customers. Much of that work was sent to Wayne's Auto Body, owned by Wayne Lee, a local businessman who had a repair shop on Gravois when Dave owned a Toyota dealership on Lindbergh. In 1999, Dave Mungenast, Dave, Jr. and Ray acquired 80% of Wayne's Auto Body, asking Lee to stay on to run the business. Lee explains, "I was asked to stay five years, and I agreed to three. I stayed under contract for a fourth year, and now it has been seven years and there is no discussion of a contract. I've known Dave for 40 years, and there has never been an angry word or a misunderstanding. We opened at a second location in 2001, and we both seem to be comfortable with how things are going." Unlike other Mungenast businesses, the body shop has not been rebranded with the Mungenast name. Dave explains, "Wayne's already had a strong reputation with positive brand recognition, and we saw no benefit in interfering with that."

Like his brothers and his father, Dave Mungenast, Jr. is an outdoorsman and a skilled off-road motorcycle rider. However, his personal passion is professional bass fishing, and he has pursued that sport as energetically as his father pursed motorcycle endurance competition. Dave, Jr. fished competitively from 1993 through 2003, retiring at last to devote more time to business and his growing family. Like his father, he looked for an opportunity to earn a living in the sport he loves. Starting by buying a small storefront boat dealership at Osage Beach, Missouri near Lake of the Ozarks in 1998, the Mungenasts moved the business to lakeside in 2000 to establish Dave Mungenast Yacht Club Marina. The facility, featuring a newly-constructed watercraft dealership, a full-service repair shop, and 100 covered slips up to 50 feet in length, required major earth removal and enormous investment. The business offers a full line of fishing and pleasure craft, in addition to personal watercraft.[3]

[2] More information about Classic Motorcycles LLC can be found on the Internet at http://www.classicmotorcyclesllc.com/.

[3] More information about the Mungenast family of businesses, including all dealerships and the auto body company, can be found at http://www.davemungenast.com/en_US/.

Dave with George H.W. and Barbara Bush.

In 2005, under the direction of Dave, Jr. and manager Tim Bonagurio, Dave Mungenast Motor Sports was totally renovated. The business has outlived most of the brands it once sold, and today is an exclusive Honda dealership. However, in addition to motorcycles it also offers Honda power products, all-terrain vehicles, and personal watercraft. Unlike many early Honda dealers, Dave, Sr. has not turned his back on the roots of his success. Others who made good money selling motorcycles took on car franchises, abandoned their motorcycle business, joined the country club set, and behaved like they were too good to have anything to do with motorcycling. To the contrary, Dave has never hidden the fact that he loves motorcycles and is proud of his affiliation with them. When Mungenast was elected chairman of the American International Automobile Dealers Association in 1998, to open the organization's annual convention, he rode a motorcycle

Dave with President Ronald Reagan.

onto the stage. And how many other automobile dealers do you know who will place a top-of-the-line Honda sport touring motorcycle in his Acura or Lexus showroom?

By the late 1980s, Dave Mungenast was no longer running his businesses as a day-to-day crisis. Success and financial stability had allowed him to start managing. His sons, after adequate professional training, were carrying much of the management load, and his longtime veterans, including Dave Larsen, Patty Ramsey, Don Levin, and others were functioning as a well-oiled machine. Dave had been using the services of a CPA named

Lyman Henson since 1975, and in 1979 the Mungenast tax and financial management work was turned over to Henson's 23-year-old son, Steve. Over the years, Steve Henson—while not a Mungenast employee—has become an integral member of the team, helping Dave set financial priorities for a large network of enterprises that includes dealerships, commercial property, and philanthropy. Henson, who works closely with Dave and his sons on all business acquisitions, says, "Dave Mungenast researches his opportunities very carefully to minimize risk, but he also has vision. He has an uncanny way of looking deeper into opportunities than anyone else I know. I have learned not to advise Dave too strongly. One time I persuaded him not to go into a business deal, and it became a big opportunity lost. Everything I told him at the time was correct, but the situation soon changed, and I think Dave was able to envision that. Still, he followed my advice and lost out. I will never again advise him NOT to do something. I'll give him the numbers as I see them, but I will not get in the way of Dave following his intuition."

To keep things running smoothly, and to provide marketing, human resources, and data processing services for all of the individual businesses, Dave Mungenast has created an umbrella management company known as ManCo. His brother Tom, who had recently retired from an executive position with Sears handling labor relations and human resources, helped set up ManCo and worked for a time to set up its personnel and business systems. Many of the senior employees work for ManCo, and members of the Mungenast family are its officers. With Dave Mungenast, customer service began on the sales floor of his small motorcycle dealership in 1965 as a matter of personal style and philosophy. Through ManCo, customer service has become a science, built around a sophisticated system for surveying and tracking customer satisfaction created by Tom Herring, an Army veteran with experience at a car dealership in Florida, then with the National Automobile Dealers Association, who joined the Mungenast organization in 1988. Herring, now deceased, was a specialist in statistics and reporting, and created the ground floor for what would become known as the "PR Department," a center where data is developed and organized to evaluate customer satisfaction and compare the various dealerships on a systematic basis. Today, the department is run by skilled and experienced personnel under the direction of Tina Yeager. Yeager, from the small town of Gray Summit, Missouri is another example of long-

Dave and Barbara with the Dick Gephardts and President Bill Clinton.

time service, growth, and loyalty within the Mungenast organization. She explains, "Don Levin hired me as a part-time receptionist. I planned to be here two years to pay off my college debt, then probably go back to Gray Summit. I was just a small-town girl who felt so unsophisticated and out of place in the big city, but Dave and his people treated me like I was really important."

Yeager, time would prove, turned out to be important indeed. With only a year on the job, she was assigned to Herring and directed to collect and review data provided by the salesmen. Tina recalls, "The salesmen were generating logs every day, and I was asked to review and analyze them and report any trends, problems, or opportunities I might see." She smiles and adds, "The salesmen hated me because they knew I was always looking over their shoulders, and I was always asking them questions to clarify things in the logs." She continues, "We had a lot of information that we were doing nothing with, and in some areas we needed to know more." With these findings in hand, Tom Herring created a public relations department consisting of individuals who would use the sales and service logs to call customers and potential customers to inquire about their experience

Dave with Senator Bob Dole.

and level of satisfaction. Today, Yeager supervises a staff of four full-time and six part-time employees who spend all their time on the phones, contacting every customer on a regular basis, including the customers of the auto body shops. Yeager says, "We have callers who have gotten to know the names of the kids of the people they are calling. It is like they are family friends, and this gives the dealerships a very friendly and personal touch." As the system grew, special software was developed to speed up data processing and generate reports that are distributed to store managers on a daily basis. Not only can managers better track the performance of their salespersons, but the sales people also benefit by gaining a finer understanding of what their customers need.

Furthermore, the ManCo system has been integrated with the statistical quality control systems provided by all of the brands, including Honda, Toyota, Acura, and Lexus. Customer satisfaction analysis has reached such a level at ManCo that one might think it a carefully-guarded trade secret. At such a suggestion, Don Levin laughs, "We'll bring any competitor in here any time to see what we are doing. We have done this, and they walk

Dave's right arm in his business empire, Patty Ramsey, with Ed Schmidt, former employee and fellow Six Days rider.

away shaking their heads. They're just not willing to invest the time and money in the kind of system we have developed over the last 20 years." He adds, "There are services where dealers can outsource their telephone research, but it just isn't the same. When you know the names of your customer's kids and what grade they are in and where they went to camp last summer, no outsourced operation is going to come close to what Tina and her staff can do."

Dave Mungenast is not a computer geek. The closest he gets to E-mail is when Patty Ramsey prints one out and places it on his desk. However, he is a big believer in data, systems, and communication. He can analyze one of the customer satisfaction printouts as insightfully and quickly as any of the more than 450 employees in his organization, and he strongly encourages investment in any technology that will improve its relationship with his customers. To keep this large organization in focus and moving in the right direction, Dave has created a Tuesday morning management meeting attended by all of the dealership managers, Dave's three sons, who are vice presidents of ManCo; and the key ManCo employees, including Levin, Yeager, director of accounting and systems administrator Vatia Flach, and others.

Dave with Soichiro Honda upon Honda's induction into the United States Automotive Hall of Fame in Detroit in 1969

Sales figures are tracked against goals, customer satisfaction statistics are reviewed, problems are aired, personnel needs are analyzed, and plans for the upcoming week, month, and quarter are discussed. Under leadership of the sons, each of the dealerships has developed its own personality consistent with the image of the brand, but also colored by individual style. Sometimes vigorous debate will take place, and at these moments Dave, Sr. will sit quietly and listen carefully to each individual who expresses his or her view. Eventually, Dave speaks and the room will listen.

Tom Heininger, Dave's longtime friend who built Webco, one of the most successful and prestigious brands of motorcycle performance accessories of the 1960s and 1970s, has watched Dave in group situations, and says, "Dave listens a lot and says little. But finally, when he speaks, you can feel a calming effect descend over the whole room. He can bring a group together and an issue into focus with a single sentence, or even just with a question." Heininger adds, "Dave runs his companies like the conductor of a big symphony." Indeed, Dave has surrounded himself with brilliant talent, which he has further developed through a heavy investment in education and training. Each plays his or her role expertly, and would stand out in any business environment, but within the Mungenast operation they are able to perform as an organized, complex, and greater whole under Dave's skilled but light-handed direction. Within Mungenast's large orchestra, Dave Larsen, Don Levin, and Patty Ramsey deserve to be singled out as first chair performers. The elaborate business organization might not exist today had it not been for their attention to detail during the era of Dave's careers in international motorcycle competition and motion picture stunt work. Larsen handled the motorcycle business, Levin managed the automobile dealerships, and Ramsey functioned as a personal assistant and handled paperwork for all the stores. Ramsey came to job in 1973, the weekend after her high school graduation. Though she left in 1987 for the birth of a daughter, she returned in 1990 and has been there since, serving for the last 15 years as Dave's personal assistant. She recalls, "When I came to work, I did not even see Dave for the first three weeks. He was off riding the Six Days somewhere." Among her diverse duties, she read movie scripts and sometimes babysat Kurt by letting him help answer the phones. In fact, within the Mungenast orchestra, Ramsey might be described as First Violin. Barbara Mungenast confirms, "There is just no estimating Patty's value to Dave and the organization. She is resourceful, on the spot, and always so willing to help. As the only person who knows all of Dave's movements at any given moment, she is the person who helps him get the most from his time and resources. He would be lost without her."

In addition to chairing the formal weekly meetings of ManCo, Dave Mungenast is a skilled practitioner of management by walking around. Unlike some successful businessmen who declare their status and reinforce their authority with jewelry, luxury cars, and a showcase office, Dave arrives daily in a pickup truck, usually wearing jeans, an open neck shirt, and sneakers. He wears a Rolex watch, but it is a generations-old stainless steel model. His office is not a spacious room at the Acura or Lexus store, but tucked away in an upstairs corner of the pre-owned Honda dealership. It is small and cluttered with pho-

tographs and memorabilia, providing a comfortable den where Dave can review his mail and return phone calls. With his sons and competent managers running the day-to-day activity, much of Dave's time these days is devoted to his philanthropic pursuits or his service on the boards of non-profit organizations. After dealing with what Ramsey has placed on his desk, Dave is apt to wander down into the showroom, through the service department, then across the parking lot to the Honda new car dealership. He may visit the motorcycle store, or drive over to Classic Motorcycles on Gravois. Or he may take a drive out to Manchester to walk through the Acura and Lexus dealerships. During these forays, Dave chats with employees at every level of the chain of command. His memory for names, current personal circumstances, and the names of family members is astonishing. He treats employees with deference and courtesy, as if each employee were a member of his own family. He may quietly and tactfully offer a bit of advice from time to time, but if he sees a problem he will never directly involve himself or confront an employee. Rather, at a later date he will work through his own chain of command to find a solution, and each solution will be consistent with the goal of maintaining customer satisfaction.

The organization's dogged pursuit of one-on-one personal relationships with customers has brought a surprising secondary benefit that no one would have anticipated 20 years ago when Herring and Yeager started analyzing logs and most auto dealers were acting the fool in their television commercials. Today, the Mungenast dealerships spend practically no money on advertising! Through satisfied customers, their growth continues to be driven by repeat business and new customer referrals. Dave, Jr. explains, "About the only advertising we do is when there is a co-op promotion where the manufacturer is paying so much of the cost that it would be foolish for us not to participate." Rather, in their attention to customers, ManCo has used part of what otherwise might be an advertising budget to support a direct mail program managed by Don Levin through which all clients regularly receive a newsletter telling what's happening at the Mungenast family of businesses. The organization has developed a database of 40,000 names, and continuous contact with current and previous customers has resulted in extraordinarily high repeat sales, known as "customer retention." whereas most automobile dealers would be happy with 30 percent customer retention, the Mungenast dealerships achieve as high as 65 to 70 percent.

Those businesses have grown exponentially because Dave Mungenast is a self-taught and dedicated proponent of fair dealing and customer satisfaction. He agrees with the philosophy of Texas auto dealer and author Carl Sewell who has calculated that a single lifelong, well-treated customer can be worth over $300,000.[4] Sewell arrives at this conclusion by reckoning that an individual may buy a dozen cars in a lifetime, based on the assumption that an average automobile price is $25,000. It sounds like a theoretical exercise, not likely to happen in real life. However, the Mungenast dealerships have proven the theory, and have sold more than a dozen automobiles to a single, satisfied, dedicated customer. Or, perhaps a policy of customer satisfaction can even exceed valuation in dollars. For example, how do you place a value on the fact that a city alderman is happy that thirty years ago you sold him a motorcycle?

[4] Carl Sewell and Paul B. Brown, "Customers for Life: How to Turn That One-Time Buyer into a Lifetime Customer," Pocket Books, a division of Simon & Schuster, Inc., 1990, page 162.

CHAPTER EIGHT

Barbara Mungenast: Wife, Mother, Grandmother, Artist

Barbara in high school, 1956.

Barbara McAboy was born June 10, 1938, the second of three sisters, and raised just north of Tower Grove Park in South St. Louis. Her Scots-Irish family was of modest means, and except for one uncle, Barbara was the first to earn a high school diploma. Personable, vivacious, energetic, self-reliant, and popular, she belonged to an exclusive sorority, worked sales and secretarial jobs from the time she was old enough to be hired, and had her own apartment and automobile—which she describes as "a cute, little '52 Chevy"—which she acquired shortly after graduating high school. After graduation, she went to work for the Missouri Pacific railroad. Barbara recalls, "I was very ambitious. I had no idea about the existence of gender bias on the job; what people later started calling the 'glass ceiling.'" She continues, "I saw a good job posting at Missouri Pacific that I was qualified for, and I applied. Suddenly, I found myself sitting in an office full of

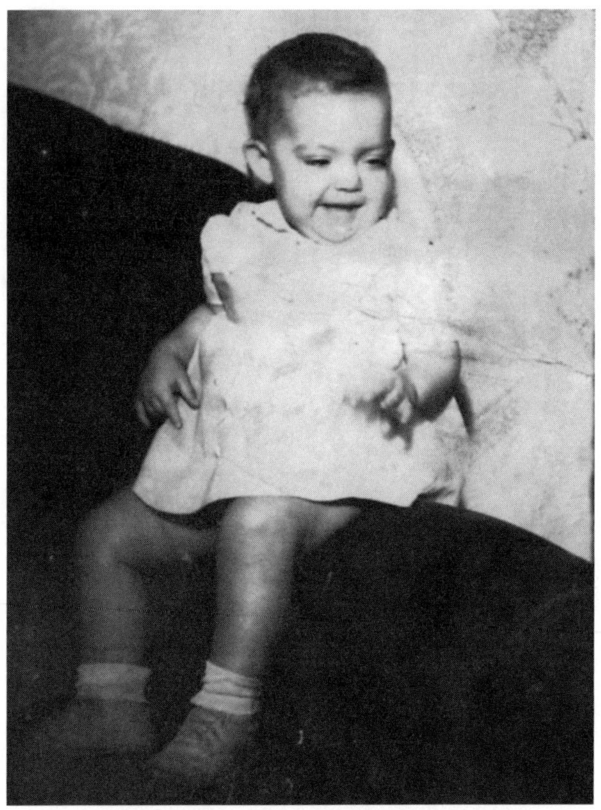

Barbara Jean McAboy at 18 months.

high-ranking men. They inquired about why I wanted the job and seemed embarrassed to discuss it. I learned later that it was a job that no woman had ever held or applied for, and they simply didn't know how to deal with me. I had shaken up the system without intending to do so, just by pursuing what seemed to me like a normal career." Still, Missouri Pacific valued her work, and after her first son, David, was born on April 1st, 1960, they kept her on company benefits through the birth of her second son, Ray, who was born on July 17 1961, despite the fact that she actually never returned to the job. After Ray's birth, she decided being a mother was job enough.

Ray's arrival proved an exciting event for the Mungenasts. Barbara explains, "I almost waited too long. I knew I was in labor, but David, Jr. was only 15 months old, and I wanted to stay with him as long as possible. Dave was pretty agitated and kept demanding that we depart for the hospital. We had a little Volkswagen, and I started wondering if I was going to deliver in the car. When we got to the hospital, Dave snatched me up and went

Barbara at Forest Park, age three.

running in with me in his arms. I can remember riding up in an elevator and this nun behind me kept pushing down hard on my shoulders and telling me to sit in a wheel chair. I was getting really angry because I could not sit down because Ray was already on the way. There was a great panic when they got me to the delivery room to discover that Ray was already coming into the world." The year after Ray's arrival, the growing family moved from St. Louis and built a house at Lake Montowese, south of the city.

After launching his motorcycle dealership in 1965 and his first automobile sales venture the following year, Dave was often absent, preoccupied with building the businesses and pursuing his career as an international motorcycle endurance rider. What at first appeared to be easy money from booming motorcycle sales in 1965 quickly turned to a struggle by 1967, thanks to social and economic problems arising from the escalating war in Vietnam. Credit became scarce for both businessmen and their customers. Barbara recalls, "It was a difficult time. We had two little boys at home, the businesses were in jeopardy, and there

Barbara and Dave at their first home at Lake Montowese, 1962.

wasn't much money to spare." Barbara devoted her energy to creating a good home for her young boys while Dave focused on building the business.

Lake Montowese was a small community in a beautiful, rural environment. Barbara recalls, "Everyone knew their neighbors and it was a safe place for children to play and enjoy the out-of-doors." Although a lot had changed since Dave Mungenast's childhood days as an aspiring trapper and mountaineer, Lake Montowese provided some of the opportunities for his sons that he had enjoyed in the countryside. Barbara recalls the time when she and the children came upon two orphaned red-tailed hawks. She says, "The boys and I watched them and talked about them all day long, wondering when the parents would return." When it became clear that the young hawks had been abandoned, young David took charge of the rescue. Barbara recalls, "We went down to the hardware store and got materials, and we built a big cage to give the hawks as much room as possible. David—then a teenager—really worked hard on the project. The safety of the birds became his project and his responsibility, and we raised them to young adulthood before returning them to the

Barbara with David Jr, left; and Ray, right, in 1966.

wild that fall." Barbara checked out books about hawks, and she and the boys studied and learned how to take care of the birds. She says, "We were worried that raising them in captivity would spoil them, but we learned that even domesticated hawks can return immediately to the wild. That told us we were doing the right thing, so the boys felt very positive about the project."

Barbara became deeply involved in the community. She says, "Lake Montowese was like a village. It was a place you wanted to invest time and energy in because it was worth it." Barbara became vice president of the property owners' association and chair of the garden committee, which was responsible for keeping the commons groomed and looking nice. In addition to her tasks as a mother and community leader, Barbara continued to pursue her education, attending night school at Jefferson College. In this process, she awakened an inherent talent that had long been dormant. In 1968, the year third son Kurt was born, Barbara took a class in pastels, and it became a revelation. She says, "I've always had an interest in art. As a small girl, I would draw and color on grocery sacks. But I had never experienced anything like pastels, the way they would blend and flow." Barbara began to dedicate herself to developing her talent, and Dave presented her a gift of her first set of paints and art supplies.

Dave's uncle, Carl Bokel, was a successful interior designer who worked for a fine furniture store in St. Louis and consulted

Barbara with her early wildlife paintings.

its clients in design and furniture selection. Barbara had always been interested in design, and Bokel became her mentor, teaching her some of the principles and techniques of interior design. Barbara created her own company named "Flair," and took some jobs designing interiors for condos and some office buildings. She began to collaborate with Pat Lloyd, an architect, working on the interiors of some of Lloyd's buildings. When Dave bought property on Lindbergh Avenue for his Honda automobile and motorcycle stores, Barbara found an opportunity to apply her talents to benefit the family businesses. Carl Bokel assisted with the design of the Honda automobile dealership, then Barbara designed the interior of the new motorcycle store. Next, she remodeled and updated the Honda car dealership. However, the biggest opportunity came in 1986 when Dave was selected to become one of the first fifty Acura dealers in America. The launch of a new, high-quality brand required an impressive and appealing sales environment. Architect Lloyd designed a new building for property on Manchester Road, and Barbara took full responsibility for the interior design. Their work became a benchmark for Acura, selected to illustrate one of their promotional brochures. With this successful project, Barbara's credentials as a skilled designer were well established, and when Dave became part of the launch of Lexus in 1989, Barbara was sent to Chicago to consult for the corporate design team, helping plan the style and standards to which the new Lexus dealerships would aspire. Barbara reports, "So much of Dave's time and business was outside of my sphere of activity. Designing the buildings gave us a wonderful opportunity to work together. It gave me an opportunity to become part of the growth of the businesses."

In the meantime, Barbara had continued with her fine art studies. She continued to study painting and got involved in competitive flower arranging. Flower arranging gave her an opportunity to work in a three dimensional medium, and from there she moved to sculpture. By this time, the Mungenast businesses were well established, and Dave was in the financial position to better support Barbara's career as an artist. She was able to travel to Africa, Asia, and South America to view wildlife habitats for her wildlife paintings, and she studied wildlife art under Rob Sadler and anatomy under Jerry Thomas in St. Louis. She also studied sculpture under Charles Edelman and Fritz White at the Loveland Academy of Fine Arts in Loveland, Colorado, and under Barry Johnson, an acclaimed Missouri sculptor. The relationship between the Johnsons and the Mungenasts has become especially interesting and close. After meeting Johnson, the Mungenasts discovered he was not just an artist, but a true cowboy and qualified stock breeder. Today, Johnson's studio is with his living quarters at the Mungenast ranch near Branson, Missouri, where Johnson has been hired to serve as caretaker and breeding supervisor for Dave's herd of prize longhorn cattle. "Sculpture," Barbara declares, "has become my passion. It requires so much study and concentration. It is exhausting, and I love the whole process from shaping the clay to casting the bronze. I love the atmosphere of the foundry. I love the smell and the grime and seeing the beautiful bronze sculpture emerge. For me, the long process of creating a sculpture is like the birth of a child."

Known among professional artists as B.J. Mungenast, Barbara's limited edition sculptures include "Masai," a lean and muscular Masai warrior protecting his herd, "Sometimes," a tall American cowboy for which Dave served as the anatomical model, "Sam," a sleeping family cat, and "Summertime Dream" of an adult and a child swinging on a rope into the old swimming hole, which, Barbara explains, is based on Dave, Jr. and a composite of all of their grandchildren.[1] Mungenast uses the strength of bronze to achieve a dynamic sense of motion not possible through other media. "Masai," and "Summertime Dream," for example, position their mass well off center to the base, attached at a thin point—a foot in the case of the running Masia and the dangling rope in the case of swimmers—of bronze, and creating the impression that the piece is in motion. In contrast, "Sometimes" and "Sam" depict stability in their quiet stillness.

For "Sometimes," Dave Mungenast was the model, which, Barbara says, with a smile, illustrates how far he is willing to go to support her art. She explains, "For life sculpture, you do not begin with the clothed subject. You must get the anatomy right before you give any thought to its final, clothed external appearance. If the proportions, the bone structure, the musculature are not correct, the final piece will not be right. She continues, "For 'Sometimes,' Dave posed in a Speedo swimsuit, tall boots, and a cowboy hat. So I could work when he did not have time to pose, I took photographs from every angle." Barbara took the film to the local pharmacy to have it developed, and she laughs, "You should have seen the knowing smile on the face of the lady when she handed us our prints. We must have come across as a pretty kinky pair. There's no way she would have believed my explanation!"

B.J. Mungenast, artist, is in the process of completing what is likely her life masterpiece, and is on the verge of seeing it realized in monumental proportions. Entitled, "The Old Guard," the work commemorates the service of the 3rd U.S. Army In-

[1] B.J. Mungenast's work can be reviewed in greater detail on the Internet at http://www.bjmungenast.com/.

Barbara with sculptor Barry Johnson while creating "Sometimes."

fantry Regiment, based at Fort Myer, Virginia. The 3rd Infantry Regiment supports official joint armed forces ceremonies, memorial services, and special events, and provides a brigade level command in defense of the nation's capital. It guards the White House, the Tomb of the Unknown Soldier, and provides escort for all funerals at Arlington Cemetery. Its mission is homeland defense and civil support, specifically to conduct operations to deter and defeat threats aimed at the United States. Clearly, following the tragedy of September 11 and the attendant threat of future terrorist attacks, The Old Guard has taken on a new and higher level of importance. Mungenast has memorialized The Old Guard with a proud sculpture of American fighting men from three eras. These include a Revolutionary War soldier, a World War II G.I., and a modern soldier in dress uniform. They are clustered back-to-back as if in joint defense of the nation across time, yet the piece is designed so that each soldier can be cast individually, as a singular and separate sculpture. In its execution, Mungenast has spent countless hours with models in uniforms, seeking perfection in every detail. "The Old Guard" was conceived by Colonel James Laufenburg, who was Regimental Commander during the September 11 attack, approval has been obtained for its permanent location at Fort Myer, and an effort is underway to generate the funds to complete the project. Munge-

Sculpting "Masai."

Barbara and Dave in the mid-1980s. Photo by Bob Schultz.

Barbara with her trophies, Ray, Dave Jr. and Kurt (left to right) and their wives Diana, Lisa, and Katie.

nasts's larger-than-life creation will stand over 11 feet tall in perpetuity, cast in nearly a ton of bronze. More than thirty castings will be required to create the large work, and quarter-life-size replicas of the individual solders or the great work as a whole will be available as well.

Barbara Mungenast speaks of the components of fine art, namely "balance," "scale," "proportion," and "texture," and how they must all be present and well integrated. She has begun to think of her role in similar terms, made up of the equally important components of "wife," "mother," "grandmother," and "artist." Barbara says, "My husband, my sons, and my thirteen grandchildren are my whole life." About being a grandmother, she says, "It is a little like becoming a parent again, yet you have to back off a bit. You can be there for them, but you can't get in and tell their parents how to raise them." One of the Mungenast's ways of being there is to provide opportunities for family interaction. On Halloween Dave converts a garage on their property into a haunted house. On Easter, the indoor pool at the Mungenast home is abob with plastic Easter eggs filled with

Grandmother Barbara with three grandchildren in the tub, 1993.

treats and coins. Thanksgiving and Christmas dinners are hosted at different homes, and at times all of the families gather at the ranch to explore the hills and fields of the Ozarks on all-terrain vehicles, or treat the kids to a hayride. Barbara also celebrates the arrival of each grandchild with the creation of a giant stuffed bear, and just as each child is unique, no two bears are alike. And Barbara is honoring the grandchildren by sculpting a likeness of each.

Barbara's big bears. Each new grandchild is welcomed to the world with a giant custom-made stuffed bear.

Barbara Mungenast in 2001.

Dave Mungenast claims that a good marriage is one where each person can allow his or her mate to be the best they can be, and he believes that Barbara has embodied that quality. He says, "There were plenty of times when I risked everything by going into debt again to pursue a new business opportunity, and she might have stopped me if she had applied enough pressure. But she didn't do that. She always had the faith to let me do my best and be my best, even when it wasn't the safest thing to do." Yet, there is one level of business risk that Barbara Mungenast will not abide, and that is the risk of breaking the ties that bind her family.

Though the Mungenast businesses are kept on course at ManCo's weekly Tuesday morning meeting, there is another periodic meeting that is even more important. Once a month, the Mungenasts only—Dave, Barbara, Dave, Jr.; Ray, and Kurt—all sit down for a private family luncheon. At that time, the existing businesses and new opportunities are evaluated from the family's point of view. Activities or opportunities that could damage the relationship between the sons are not accepted, and it is Barbara who understands the business from this point of view. One of Dave's longtime associates says, "Barbara is the most powerful person in the Mungenast organization." Barbara scoffs at this idea. She no longer involves herself in the design and décor of the dealerships, nor does she interfere, or even inquire about profit or loss or day-to-day activities. However, on the highest strategic and philosophical level, there is no doubt her influence is supreme. If a situation arises that may be good for business but bad for the family, family will trump business every time. Barbara's job is to make sure it is so.

Among a tastefully-arranged montage of family photographs in a hallway of the Mungenast home, there is a framed parchment that declares:

In this home
We belive in living deeply,
Laughing often, and loving always.
We believe we were brought together
To support and care for each other.
We believe in celebrating together
Our faith, our heritage, our traditions.
We believe that everyone's feelings count
And that the uniqueness of each of us
Strengthens all of us.
We believe in the power of forgiveness to heal
And the power of love
To carry us through.
We believe in one another,
In this family,
In this home,
The Mungenasts.

CHAPTER NINE

The Legacy: David, Ray, and Kurt

David, Ray, and Kurt in 1971.

When David Mungenast, Jr. was born on April 1, 1960, Dave and Barbara Mungenast had very little they could call their own. They were living with Dave's parents and holding down three jobs between them while Dave was trying to earn a college degree. Then Ray arrived less than fifteen months later, on July 17, 1961. By mid-decade, Dave had decided to go into business for himself with his Honda motorcycle dealership, and by the end of the 1960s he was struggling to maintain the motorcycle shop and build an automobile dealership with little more than the day-to-day equity he could bring in through the cash register. When Kurt arrived on October 15, 1968, the Mungenasts had still not yet secured their future. They had moved in 1962 to a more comfortable and child-friendly environment at Lake Montowese, but Dave's business struggles would continue for yet another decade before he could establish himself as the largest Honda automobile dealer in St. Louis. Kurt would be ready to

The Mungenast home at Lake Montowese where David, Ray, and Kurt grew up.

graduate from high school before the Mungenast enterprise had become strong enough to be selected by Acura in 1986 as one of the nation's first fifty dealers.

It was never Dave Mungenast's goal to be just a large automobile dealer. He wanted to be the right kind of dealer. He was always aware that many do not view auto dealers as highly ethical, either toward their customers or their employees, and it was his goal to overcome this stereotype by building a business that would thrive and grow based on its reputation alone. Dave says, "I wanted automobile dealerships where my employees would be proud to have their own children come to work there." His own sons would be the test for the measurement of that success, since that sentiment would apply to them as well.

In Dave Mungenast's teenage years, motorcycles were a vehicle often used to express rebellion and irresponsibility. By the time the Mungenasts had children of their own, motorcycles had become their bread and butter, and Dave and Barbara discovered how they could become a vehicle to teach responsibility to their sons. Barbara explains, "At the age of eight, each of the boys was given a new mini-cycle, but that was the last motorcycle they were ever given, even though we were in the business." The boys were also given a helmet and proper protective riding gear and taught how to use it. Dave showed them how to clean and maintain their motorcycles, how to adjust the chain, and how to make repairs. These skills would become important to the boys, because their little motorcycles were their personal equity. When they decided they were ready for a larger one, Dave would show them how to detail the bike and make it as presentable as possible, then it would be put up for sale among the used motorcycles at the dealership. What money a Mungenast son could get for his motorcycle would be applied to his purchase of the next one, but he had to come up with the difference from his own pocket. For this, all of the boys were taught at an early age to do chores, and they were allowed to earn money by sweeping up and doing odd jobs at the Honda motorcycle store on Saturdays. Ray Mungenast recalls, "At the peak, there were over twenty kids in the neighborhood with motorcycles, and it was not just because Dad was a motorcycle dealer. Other parents saw how our family functioned and how the motorcycle became a tool for good development and good family relationships."

Lake Montowese is a self-managed, unincorporated community of about a hundred homes located in a wooded environment along a single road circling a 55 acre lake in Jefferson county, about 30 miles south of St. Louis. It was a relatively safe environment for young children because traffic traveled in only one direction on the road that circled the lake. In addition, to keep the kids off the road as much as possible, they were given a section of the woods where they were allowed to establish trails for their off-road motorcycles. Dave, Jr. recalls, "It was pretty much a perfect place for a kid. We went to a rural public school, and after school the bus would drop us off at the entrance of the property. It was about a mile walk to the house, and we were always surrounded by nature with the woods on one side and the lake on the other. We were expected to finish our homework and chores, then we could get on our bikes and ride until dark. There were 20 or 25 kids in the community with motorcycles, and we practically rode the wheels off of them." Barbara adds, "We knew there was a certain amount of danger involved, but we thought it was a lot better than the risks of growing up in the city. It took the boys about 20 minutes to make a loop through the woods on their motorcycles, so I taught them to always make a pass by the house after a loop through the woods. This way I could keep tabs on them. It all became part of the fun. I could hear young David coming up the road, and when he passed the house he would pop a long wheelie and wave at me when he went by. It was just incredible how quickly their riding skills developed. All three be-

Young David and Ray ride their Honda minibikes on the trails at Lake Montowese.

came excellent riders." About Lake Montowese, Ray says, "It may have lacked some of the advantages of city life, but there were a lot of nice things for a kid to do. In addition to trail riding, we also had the lake for fishing and swimming, and, though our parents probably never knew it, we even did a little hunting in the woods." He adds, "I think going to a large rural public school was also good for us. It included some real diversity in terms of incomes and classes of people. I think we all relate well to a wide

David and Barbara Mungenast with their legacy, David, Kurt, and Ray in 1984.

range of people, which is important in how well we do our business. I believe we learned a lot of this skill from the type of country school we attended."

By the time he was eight, Dave, Jr. was working at the Honda motorcycle dealership, cleaning up and helping out. As a teenager, even before he was licensed to drive, he would ride his trail bike the 30 miles to St. Louis. He recalls, "In those days, you could make the whole trip through the countryside, right up to the back of the dealership on Lindbergh, without ever getting on a public road." In 1978, Dave—always with his dog Jake along—began driving the company parts truck for the various dealerships, a job that he seemed to be content with for more than five years. Dave, Sr. recalls, "David did not want to go to college, and I started wondering if he was going to drive that truck for the rest of his life. Then, one day we were at the Honda dealership talking about the future, and I asked him what he wanted to do. Right out of the blue, he said, 'Dad, I want your job. I want to run all this!'"

Like his father who went away to the service and came back a different man, David appeared to mature suddenly. He says, "I'm not so different from my father. I was not the easiest teenager to live with. I had to be reminded of the boundaries pretty often. I moved out of the house at 20 and didn't pay a lot of attention to what my parents tried to teach me. But I could see that Dad was getting overwhelmed trying to run the business on his own, and one day I decided it was time to get serious." Mungenast responded by sending David to the National Automobile Dealers Association Academy in 1984 for management training, and in 1986 named him general manager of the Honda store. It was a welcome respite, because Dave, Sr.'s time was occupied with launching one of the first Acura dealerships in America. Again, like his father, it is likely that the right woman played a role in the changes in Dave, Jr.'s life, because the year before going to the NADA Academy, David had met Lisa Wibbenmeyer, whom he would marry a few years later after having established himself in the family business.

Despite the fact that he was raised with motorcycles and is an excellent rider, Dave, Jr. did not follow his father into international competition. Dave Larsen says, "Dave could have easily qualified to ride the Six Days. He is scary fast in the woods—as good as or better than anyone in the family—but he chose a different hobby." The hobby Dave, Jr. chose was fishing, which he learned from his grandfathers Andy Mungenast and Ray McAboy. Barbara says, "It was not easy being Dave Mungenast's first son. He had a lot to live up to, and he even had his father's name. It is too easy for people to make comparisons, and I think it is understandable that he sometimes chose to go his own way." By the time he was 30, Dave, Jr. was fishing professionally, and he continued for ten years. He says, "I quit competitive fishing in 2003 because I was spending so much time with the business and I did not want to be away from my family. Dad was away a lot when he was building the business, and I didn't want it to be that way." He adds, "But I still enjoy fishing for relaxation, and David, my oldest son, has become my fishing partner." Through competitive fishing, Dave, Jr. learned the sport at a depth that would eventually enable the Mungenasts to expand their motorsports enterprise into marina ownership.

Ray came along only 15 months after David. Barbara says, "Ray had an older brother to follow. A child can learn a lot by watching a sibling, and he never had the pressure of being the

Ray, riding on the American team at the International Six Days Trial.

'junior' in the family." Ray also got involved in motorcycles, riding with his brother in the woods at Lake Montowese. In addition, he had a natural athletic ability. Barbara recalls, "He was always quick, agile, and had good timing." However, he was small, which caused his mother to impose limits on his athletic endeavors. Barbara explains, "Ray was so fast and agile, he was always in demand as a running back on the kids' football teams, but I would not allow it because most of the others his age were so much bigger. They would have creamed him!" Rather, Ray excelled in track and field and as a cross-country runner, twice becoming a varsity letterman in each discipline. He qualified twice for the state finals in cross country, twice for state indoor track and field competition, and earned seventeen individual medals. In his last two years of high school he began to campaign the International Six Days qualifiers, and in 1981, at the age of 20, qualified for the U.S. team to ride at the Isle of Elba. He qualified also for the next four years, riding in Czechoslovakia, Wales, Holland, and Spain, finishing every event to earn two bronze and three silver medals. Dave and Barbara joined him for the events in Italy and Wales, serving as members of the American support team. During his last two years of international competition, Ray also competed in national endurance events at the AA level, which is the highest level of proficiency. Ray relates, "It was something I always aspired to do. When Dad was riding the Six Days, Leroy Winters and the Penton clan would stay at our house when they were traveling to the qualifiers. These people were my idols, and I grew up wanting to do what they did.

Ray might have had a longer Six Days career, except for the arrival of new opportunities in his father's growing organization. Ray had been learning the family business by working for Dave Larsen at the Honda motorcycle dealership, and eventually became its general manager. He says, "I was always around motorcycles and comfortable with that business. I was not sure I wanted to be in the car business until I was about 30." When Dad opened the Lexus franchise, Don Levin was promoted to run it, and Ray was offered the management of the Acura store. He says, "I hoped to ride the Six Days a few more times, but I was taking classes at St. Louis University and working over 40 hours a week, and I consulted with my parents and we agreed that it was time to terminate the international motorcycle career." However, his involvement in motor sports did not end entirely, because from 1991 through 1993 Ray raced a Honda CRX under the auspices of the Sports Car Club of America. He won three national championship events and on one occasion teamed up with Taz Harvey for the 24 Hours of Mosport. Ray recalls, "We were doing very well, then another driver on our team wrecked the car during the night." About his racing style, Ray explains with a smile, "I learned to race riding motocross, and it probably made me a little too aggressive in the first corner. I didn't see anything at all wrong with bumping and trading a little paint while jockeying for position. Other drivers would come around our pit pretty upset to remind me that this was supposed to be a gentleman's sport. I never knew what they were taking about. I was there to race!" Body shop manager Wayne Lee confirms, "More than one Monday morning I came to work to find Ray's car on its trailer in our parking lot, ready for a little more paint and body work."

While Dave, Jr. and Ray followed similar paths into the family business, for Kurt it has been quite different, due to the passage of time and change in the circumstances of the family. Kurt was born a little over seven years after Ray. By this time, the winding country road that led to Lake Montowese had been changed to a four lane highway, and a rural environment had begun to evolve toward suburbia. Changes took place in the administration of the local school system that Barbara Mungenast was not pleased with. She explains, "Kurt was a very good student. Then one day I learned from another mother that our sons had been placed in a class of underachievers with the hope they would influence better behavior and study habits. I was dumbfounded by this kind of educational philosophy. I guess a mother can be proud that her son is seen as a good role model, but a decision like this showed absolutely no regard for Kurt, his development, or his education." The small brick home at Lake Montowese had become very crowded with the growing family, and by this time Dave's Honda car store had become the top dealership in the city. Lake Montowese had been good to the Mungenast family, but the situation had changed, and, besides, they could afford more. Barbara insisted that they move closer to St. Louis where they would have access to a better school system. Dave acquired three acres in a community called Sunset View Estates in South County, not ten minutes from the Honda car and motorcycle dealerships. Though the acreage already had a house on it, Dave commissioned St. Louis architect Pat Lloyd to design a new home. Barbara assisted with the interior design. Later, after Lloyd and Barbara refurbished the house already on the property, Dave, Jr. bought it and moved into Sunset View Estates not far from his parents.

Kurt recalls, "It was really quite a change for me. Here I was this country boy from Lake Montowese in my faded bellbottoms, and suddenly we were in this beautiful home with an indoor swimming pool. I realized our family was doing pretty well." In this way, Kurt's circumstance has differed from that of his older brothers, which has been reflected in his very different path into the family business. Another change for Kurt was the fact that the American motorcycle sport had undergone a kind of revolution. Kurt, like his brothers, had honed his riding skills on the trails around Lake Montowese. But the year Kurt was born, an enterprising promoter named Edison Dye had launched a series of motocross races in America called the Inter-Am, and that

Teenage Kurt, the aspiring motocrosser.

series included a venue near St. Louis. Motocross was an exciting, fast-paced, aerobatic form of European motorcycle competition that took America by a storm. Kurt was among the young riders of his generation who became enamored with the sport. Whereas Ray had followed his father as an international off-road endurance rider, Kurt wanted to become a motocross star. The Mungenasts had acquired a ranch in Madison County, and at fourteen Kurt was operating a bulldozer, building his own motocross practice course. He was serious. He rode well and wanted to get better, taking professionally-run courses in the techniques of motocross. But his aspirations to become a motocross star ended at 16 when he shattered his leg in a crash at a motocross race in Illinois. He says, "It was a defining moment for me. It changed my life and my plans, and I still keep the pin from my leg on my desk for a paper weight as a reminder of that moment."

During his final years in high school, Kurt considered enlisting in the military. Some of the role models in his life were his uncles, Tom and Andy. Tom had fought as a Marine on Okinawa in the Second World War, and Andy became one of the most accomplished pilots in the Army Air Corps, and is still an instructor at the War College at Maxwell Air Force Base in Birmingham, Al-

Dave Sr. with Ray and Dave, Jr., circa 1980.

abama. The adults in Kurt's family, including his father, encouraged him to continue his education first, and he enrolled at St. Louis University where he completed a degree in history. In 1988, during his college years, he met his future wife Katie Zenner. Kurt received his Marine commission in January, 1991, the couple was married in May, and the following month Kurt went active. As a Marine, Kurt became a CH46 twin-rotor helicopter pilot and completed a master's degree in economics. For three and a half years he served on Okinawa. As for his plan to make the military his career, again, circumstances changed. Kurt says, "After about three deployments, we had four kids and the equipment I was flying was becoming pretty obsolete." Kurt had become devoted to his family, and his desire to be a father had begun to conflict with his obligations as a pilot. He says, "During work-ups before deployment, we would be right off-shore from Okinawa within sight of our neighborhood lights, but not able to phone home, much less visit, for weeks at a time. I remember that, and my heart goes out to those who are on deployment to Iraq for a year at a time." Kurt spoke to his father about a position in the family business. He says, "It was not a simple transition for anyone involved. We had all proceeded as if I would be in the military for the rest of my career, and my parents are not people who will just move someone out of the way to make room for one of his sons. They will not treat people that way, and they always expected all of his boys to earn everything they got." By way of example, Kurt remembers his first car and laughs, "On my 16th birthday (1984), they took me out to the driveway where they presented me a used 1978 Honda. I was thrilled, then Dad said, 'Okay, you owe the dealership $400!'"

The Mungenasts sat down and worked out a plan in which older brothers Dave and Ray became the key players. By the time Kurt left the military in 1998, they had become the managers of all of the stores, whereas Dave, Sr. had moved to an advisory role with the automobile dealerships to allow more time to focus on real estate and his volunteer work. Dave, Sr. says, "I could not appear to play favorites. David and Ray had come up through the ranks, they had earned their way, and it was they who would be the future of the business. If we were going to integrate Kurt into the plan, they were the only ones who would have the right and the ability to do it." After working for five years at St.. Louis Honda as the service manager and as a sales manager, and graduating from NADA Academy, at the end of 2003 Kurt was offered an opportunity by Dave, Jr. and Ray to oversee the Alton Toyota and Dodge operations, in addition to any future North County operations, in the role of Vice President. About the Alton responsibility Kurt says, "After coming from a large metro Honda store with 30 plus years of loyal customers, this smaller market had been a challenge. Dad was right. Getting this store to perform is more difficult than a metro store, but Mark Lemons and I and our team are doing it, thanks to what I learned from working for David and his managers, especially Ed Riley, his general sales manager."

Those who know the Mungenast sons note that they are like, but not like Dave, Sr. Each seems to have a dominant personality trait that can be recognized as something evident in Dave's personality, yet none is exactly like him. They are distinct individuals who run their businesses differently, yet strive to keep them consistent with the way of doing business that Dave has established. Ron Ribolzi, a Six Days rider contemporary with Ray who joined the organization in 1986 and has moved up the ranks to general manager of the Acura store, says, "Dave, Jr. is very analytical and numbers oriented, and focuses on the bottom

David Jr. and Lisa with family, 1989.

line. Ray has his father's people skills. Kurt is like his father when he was younger. He is a rebel, but he is also bringing good systems management and analytical skills to his job. The boys have new ideas, but their values are the same as their parents'." Like their father, each has a fondness for nature, animals, and the out-of-doors. While growing up, Dave, Jr. and Ray worked one day a week at the ranch in Madison County. Dave says, "I loved it, and I got serious about ranching." Whereas Dave, Sr's animals are a hobby, Dave, Jr. has leased land from his father and created a business raising Angus cattle. His wife Lisa maintains all the records for the business and their sons assist with the 100-head herd. Their family consists of Jessica, 17; Kristina, 16; Danielle, 14; David, 11; and Michael, 8.

Ray met his wife Diana Collins through a mutual friend at a country and western dance bar in 1992. Ray jokes, "We hit it off well right away, and it was certainly not my dancing skill that impressed her." Ray and Diana have two children, Nick, 5; and Ryan, 2; and their outdoor interests have taken the form of horse ranching. They acquired 300 acres near Huzzah, Missouri in

Ray, Diana, and children, 2004.

2003 and have since expanded it to a little over 400 acres. After renovating a 100-year-old farm house, they have begun to raise horses. Ray says, "It is a beautiful place with a brook running in front of the house and three natural springs on the property. We all enjoy riding and hope that within five years we will be breeding horses commercially."

In 2005, Kurt and Katie acquired 140 acres on the Mississippi River in Illinois where they ride ATVs and motorcycles and have planted a small vineyard and garden, and keep bees. Kurt says, "The view of the river really got to me, and it helped convince Katie to take the financial plunge." Their home is in the St. Louis suburb of Kirkwood, but on weekends the family goes to the farm. Their family consists of Caroline, 14; Joseph, 12; Peter, 10; Henry, 8; John, 4; and William, born in April 2006. Kurt recalls, "I remember when dad saw the property for the first time. I have always been self-weary around Dad with my financial decisions. I ran apartment buildings for a while to make some additional money, and I knew that he would drive by and inspect them when I wasn't there. Thank goodness, I did well with them—anyway, when Katie and I invested in our farm, I was really worried what Dad would think about it. It was a beautiful

Kurt, Katie, and family, 2006.

day, and when he looked down off the bluff and told me that he remembers watching the eagles with his parents right across the river from our farm, I knew that I had something special."

With their 13 children—so far—David, Ray, and Kurt represent the Mungenast legacy. Even now that they are adults with their own busy lives, Dave and his sons use their love of off-road riding as a family bonding practice. In addition to the periodic three-generational rides at the Mungenast ranch, whenever their schedules will allow, the sons will join Dave to ride the Colorado 500. Ben Cheatwood, a Honda employee, a professional race announcer, and a regular Colorado 500 participant relates, "I saw them here one year at the Colorado 500, and the boys reminded me of a fighter escort, clustered around the father as they rode down the trail. I started bringing my son to the Colorado 500 because of what I saw going on with Dave and his sons. It is a way to maintain and strengthen the bonds between the two generations and the love in the family." Dan Borgmeyer, an independent advertising and public relations consultant to automobile dealers who has known and worked with Dave since the mid-1970s, says, "With 80 percent of my clients today, I am dealing with the sons of dealers. The Mungenast organization is the most stable I know because the sons have adopted the values and business practices of their father. In most it is not like that. Usu-

Dave Sr., left, with Ray, Kurt, and Dave Jr., taking a break from the Colorado 500 at a restaurant in Ouray, Colorado.

ally the second generation enjoys the spoils of their father's hard work, and sometimes runs the business into the ground." Barbara Mungenast is far less analytical about the situation. She says, "Dave, Sr. has earned many awards and honors for the many achievements over his life. My trophies are my three sons and my grandchildren."

CHAPTER TEN

Philanthropy: Giving Back to the Community

Dave Mungenast was raised in a home where a high value was placed on philanthropy and community service. Andy Mungenast, his father, was charitable to a fault, giving generously of his time and money to public causes and individuals he perceived as less fortunate than himself, even to the extent that Charlotte Mungenast sometimes worried about the needs of their family. Dave recalls that his father once told him, "If you are lucky enough to earn more than you need, then give it back." It is a practice that Dave and Barbara Mungenast have followed, especially as their businesses prospered and the family became more financially able. However, the Mungenasts have gone beyond personal giving to create a culture of philanthropy throughout their organization. In addition to sharing their personal time, money, and in-kind support with many non-profit organizations, Dave Mungenast has directed the resources of his companies toward public causes, and through the Dave and Barbara Mungenast Foundation has created incentives for his employees to give back to their community. A share of annual profits from the businesses are assigned to the Foundation, then much is returned through those businesses in support of charitable giving by their employees. Each dollar an employee gives to a charitable organization is matched by the dealership where he or she is employed, then matched a second time by the Dave and Barbara

Mungenast Foundation, thereby tripling the philanthropic impact of each individual's contribution.

The organizations that Dave Mungenast, his family, and his businesses serve include the Boys' Club of St. Louis; Marygrove, an organization that serves children at risk; the St. Louis South County YM/YWCA; the International Institute of St. Louis; the St. Louis Zoo; the Lion's Club; the Polly Klaas Foundation for the prevention of child abduction; the St. Louis Food Bank; St. Anthony's Hospital; Heifer International, promoting sustainable agriculture and economic development to end world hunger; the Wheels Through Time Museum; the Motorcycle Hall of Fame Museum; and various charities supported by the Colorado 500 Off-road Ride and the Malcolm Smith Baja Adventure.[1] In fact, today Dave Mungenast will serve only on the boards of non-profit organizations. In earlier days, he was sought out to serve on the board of a bank and other for-profit enterprises.[2] Now he has no time for it due to his extensive commitment to philanthropy.

Among the many organizations he supports, perhaps Dave's favorite is the Boys Club of St. Louis, which for more than 75 years, has served as an oasis of educational and athletic opportunity in the inner city environment of South St. Louis. Serving over 4,000 youths, its 36,000 square foot facility includes a gymnasium, an exercise room with weight-lifting and aerobic exercise equipment, racketball court, and natatorium complete with grandstands and locker room facilities. Outside, its 7½ acre campus includes three baseball diamonds, which convert to football and soccer fields, plus an outdoor basketball court. While its athletic program may be its most visible service, the Club also provides three game rooms for different age groups, complete with billiards, ping-pong, board games and video games. There are also an arts and crafts room, a library/learning center, and com-

[1] Listed here are major and notable beneficiaries of the Mungenast philanthropic program. Others include the Tutwiler Clinic, the Fund for Ranken, the Gephardt Legacy Fund, the Salvation Army, St. Anthony's Hospice, the Pediatric Brain Tumor Foundation, the National Automobile Dealers Charitable Foundation, the Today & Tomorrow Fund, the Juvenile Diabetes Foundation, the Pleasanton North Rotary Fund, Easter Seals, United Way, the Leukemia Society, St. Louis Bike Park, the Polish Heritage Center, Reading is Fundamental, St. Louis University, Habitat for Humanity, the American Red Cross, the Backstoppers, and the Wild Canid Center.

[2] Dave Mungenast has served on the boards of the Mehlville Bank, Gravois Bank, Mercantile Bank, and the Mississippi Valley Advisors.

Dave helps present a check to the Reading is Fundamental Program during St. Louis Public School Career Day, circa 1990.

Barbara during a Polly Klass Foundation promotion in 2000.

Dave with some of the staff of St. Anthony's Medical Center where he serves on the board of directors.

puters for the youth. Special interest clubs are available, and discussion groups are provided. Considered a national benchmark among Boys' Clubs, the South St. Louis club has a fulltime staff of eight, headed by Executive Director Tom Wild, and is governed by a 24-member Board of Directors. Dave Mungenast has served on the Board since 1987, and is currently Secretary of the Board, a position he has held since 1993. He considers support of an organization like the Boys' Club of South St. Louis more than just charity. It is also good business. Mungenast reckons that in lost time, training, and other related costs, turnover of a single employee can cost an organization as much as $50,000. He says, "From a business executive's point of view, there is a tremendous savings and advantage in having young people available in the community who are educated, well adjusted, physically fit, and skilled at teamwork and getting along with others. This is exactly the kind of citizens that the Boys' Club helps develop at an extremely low cost to the community." He adds, "The best way to improve your business is to invest in people."

With about 40 percent of the Boys' Club's $1 million annual budget provided by United Way, it is incumbent upon members of the Board to raise over a half million a year to keep the organization going. Executive Director Tom Wild confirms that Mungenast alone generated a quarter of that sum through vari-

Dave posing with the world's largest underwear for a St. Louis Boys' Club fund raiser.

ous sources, including his sponsorship of an annual golf tournament. Golf is a game that Dave Mungenast never bothered to learn, but his sons Ray and Kurt often support the Club through participation in the tournament. Wild says, "Dave is constantly working for the Boys' Club of South St. Louis. Things would be tough for us without him. He gives both his money and his time, and Barbara often joins him for Boys' Club functions." Then Wild adds, "And he does not do it for recognition or glory. Others have urged him to become president of the Board, but he is quite happy to do what he's done for the last decade, serving as secretary." Current Board President Eugene P. Slay, Chairman and CEO of Slay Industries, states, "I am pleased that back in 1991 our Board had the foresight to elect Dave as Chairman of our annual direct mail solicitation program. Dave sees to it that we meet or exceed our goal each year." Slay adds, "Dave also logs hundreds of hours as Secretary of our Board in addition to serving on various committees. He is a true hands-on gentleman concerned about the welfare of youth."

Much of the Mungenasts' charitable work is youth oriented. Another example is Marygrove, an organization serving at-risk youth, managed by the Catholic Charities, that dates back to 1849. Originally located in South St. Louis, the organization relocated to its current 43-acre campus in Florissant, Missouri,

Dave and Barbara with Mikhail Baryshnikov at a promotion for the St. Louis Zoo.

northwest of the city, in 1967. Serving poor and economically disadvantaged young people up to age 21, Marygrove provides counseling, housing, psychiatric services, and crisis intervention. With an average of 140 children in fulltime care, its overnight emergency housing program serves more than 2,000 individuals a year. Of its $7.7 million annual budget, about $4.8 comes from government reimbursement for the social services it provides, leaving nearly $3 million that must be raised from outside sources including United Way and individual charitable contributions. Marygrove was recommended by one of Dave's business associates, and the Mungenasts began to provide significant financial support through their family foundation. For their work, Dave and Barbara were named recipients of Marygrove's James J. Eagan Award in 2004. In addition, the Ray and Kurtis Mungenast families have supported Marygrove. Sister Helen Negri, its executive director, states, "They are very humble and unassuming people who have a strong belief in helping others. In my opinion, they do this solely because they believe it is the right thing to do"[3]

[3] For more information on Marygrove on the Internet, go to http://www.ccstl.org/agency_details.php?agencyID=23.

A third example of the Mungenasts' support of youth-oriented programs is their organization-wide service to the Polly Klaas Foundation. In October, 1993, 12-year-old Polly Klaas was abducted from her home in Petaluma, California. A national search center was created, and though Polly was ultimately found dead three months later, what searchers learned became institutionalized in a non-profit foundation for the benefit of other lost or abducted children. Since then, the Polly Klaas Foundation has assisted parents and law enforcement agencies in over 6,500 searches for missing children, and in over 85 percent of the cases, children have been found and returned home safely. The organization provides case workers, distributes child safety kits for parents, hosts public events to train adults in how to protect children, and promotes public policies, such as the Amber Alert system. For the past decade, Dave Mungenast has offered his dealerships on the third Saturday in October as a site for an annual Klaas Foundation child registration and public awareness day. Tina Yeager explains, "Through St. Louis schools, over 74,000 flyers are sent home to parents who are given an opportunity to have their children finger-printed and registered by local law enforcement. Parents who bring their children are given child safety kits and advice on how to avoid abductions and what to do in the case of abduction. Typically, we will ID over 1,500 children in a day." Yeager adds, "It is serious work, but we turn it into a party. There is food and refreshments, fire trucks are brought out and put on display, and the kids are given balloons and ice cream. There is also a silent auction to raise funds for the Foundation. Basically, the dealerships are given over to the Klaas Foundation that day, all personnel are involved in the project, and we don't sell any cars."[4] Wayne DeWitt, whose friendship with Dave dates back to the days of the Dirty Dozen and Midwest Enduro Team motorcycle clubs, shows up to cook the hot dogs for the Klaas Foundation days at the dealerships. A second charitable project that operates through the dealerships is the St. Louis Food Bank. Yeager explains, "Employees are encouraged to donate to the food bank, and their donations are matched both by the dealership and the Dave and Barbara Mungenast Foundation."[5]

[4] For more information on the Polly Klaas foundation on the Internet, go to http://www.pollyklaas.org/.

[5] For more information on the St. Louis Food Bank on the Internet, go to http://stlfoodbank.org/.

Dave and Barbara Mungenast are also major supporters of the South County YM/YWCA. One of 20 YMCA branches in greater St. Louis, South County's is a 55,000 square foot facility that includes two indoor pools, a double-court gymnasium, an indoor running track, separate family and adult locker rooms, sauna and steam rooms, a racquetball court, a nursery, an outdoor track, and a comprehensive fitness center. The city-wide system raises $2.6 million a year for scholarships, to which South County's contribution is about ten percent. Dave has served on the Board of Advisors since 1998 and is the biggest single contributor to the scholarship fund. Mel Elliott, Vice President for the Greater St. Louis YMCAs says, "Dave's fund-raising influence goes far beyond his personal contributions. He is a Pied Piper; people want to follow his lead and his example." Elliott, who is Mungenast's friend, believes he knows him well enough to understand his motives. He explains, "Dave believes his success has come from the community, and he wants to give it back through support of good causes. I think Dave feels blessed, and he does not take his success lightly. Rather, that success has instilled in him a sense of responsibility to create opportunities for others." Elliott adds, "Dave is not a man who believes you use people to acquire money. He believes you use money to care about people." Dave and Barbara are members of the Lamplighter Society, which consists of individuals who have contributed to the St. Louis YMCA endowment.[6]

An important community organization that traces its roots to the YWCA is the International Institute of St. Louis, founded in 1919. In 1910, the National Board of the YWCA created the Department of Immigration and Foreign Communities, whose mission is to oversee community institutes created to serve the foreign-born. These International Institutes provide comprehensive adjustment services, moving new Americans quickly from overwhelming dependence to productivity and self-sufficiency, helping them become productive, contributing participants to their neighborhoods, schools, churches, and communities as a whole. We have already noted the historical fact that St. Louis is a city that has drawn its vitality primarily from immigration (significantly German in the mid-19th century), rather than western migration of American-born folk. The Mungenasts, who trace

[6] For more information on the YMCA of Greater St. Louis on the Internet, go to http://www.ymcastlouis.org/home.html.

their roots to these 19th century German emigrants, saw the phenomenon repeat itself during their lifetime as South City fell into decline, then was revitalized within the last decade by an influx of industrious, family-centered, and community-minded Bosnians. Dave is proud of the renewal that has taken place along Gravois Road, which includes the home of his first automobile dealership, now renovated and turned into his Classic Motorcycles LLC museum, and he attributes this revival in part to the Bosnians who have moved into the neighborhood. It is little wonder then that Dave and Barbara Mungenast have chosen to support the International Institute of St. Louis through their Foundation.[7]

Beyond the Boys' Club and the YMCA, the organization that demands the greatest portion of Mungenast's volunteer energy is St. Anthony's Medical Center, a $370 million, Franciscan-affiliated institution located on the southern outskirts of the city, just midway between the Mungenast home and their Lindbergh Road dealerships.[8] Tom Rockers, St. Anthony's chief executive officer, explains Mungenast's contribution to its Board of Directors: "Dave brings to the board community understanding. He understands the needs of the community, the values of this institution, and he keeps hammering these home with consistency and conviction. When he speaks, others listen." Rockers adds, "He brings balance to the Board. Dave is a man who can relate to the president of an international automobile company, or to one of the housekeepers on our staff. He is comfortable with anyone, and he makes everyone else comfortable."

While most of Dave and Barbara Mungenast's philanthropic work is community-based and related—directly or indirectly—to the well-being of young people, it will come as no surprise that some is connected with Dave's first love, motorcycling. We have already noted his support of an orphanage in Mexico and the economically distressed communities of the western slope of Colorado through the Malcolm Smith Baja Adventure and Wally Dallenbach's Colorado 500 Off-road Ride, respectively. Malcolm Smith's Motorsports Foundation, created in 2002, is the primary benefactor of El Oasis, an orphanage where the Foundation has

[7] For more information on the International Institute of St. Louis on the Internet, go to http://www.intlinst.org/.

[8] For more information on St. Anthony's on the Internet, go to http://www.stanthonysmedcenter.com/.

installed electricity, wells, and irrigation, planted trees, built an education center, and helped expand the facility's capacity from a single dormitory to a complex containing a hundred beds.[9] Smith says, "Dave has been on all of my Baja rides but one, and he always gives generously." However, Smith also speaks of a contribution that goes beyond money. About Mungenast he says, "Dave is motivated by a challenge, and he is not afraid of risk. Dave taught me how to take bigger risks."

Wally Dallenbach's Colorado 500 can be regarded the grandfather of celebrity charity motorcycle rides. Now in its 31st year, the event has distributed over $1.1 million to more than a hundred schools, charities, ministries, and social service organizations in the small communities of Colorado's western slope.[10] Dave Mungenast is an enthusiastic participant in the ride, and when their busy schedules can be coordinated, he and his sons use the event for some quality time together. Colorado 500 co-founder Wally Dallenbach says, "Dave came to the Colorado 500, we rode together a lot, and we hit it off. He has good morals and his priorities are right. He is a family man and was a hard racer in his day. He worked hard, raced hard, raised a family, and now he uses his abilities to support good works." Dallenbach adds, "And the kids are all great. They have stuck with him and they share his values." In his love on nature and off-road motorcycling, Mungenast is also a contributor to the Blue Ribbon Coalition, a non-profit advocacy organization that supports access and multiple use of public lands.[11]

Beyond his own collection of vintage and antique motorcycles at Classic Motorcycles LLC in St. Louis, Mungenast also supports two other leading motorcycle museums, the Motorcycle Hall of Fame Museum, based in Pickerington, Ohio, and the Wheels Through Time Museum, located in Maggie Valley, North Carolina. The Motorcycle Hall of Fame Museum was founded at American Motorcyclist Association headquarters in Westerville, Ohio in 1990, then moved to a larger facility in Pickerington, Ohio in 1999. Himself a member of the Motorcycle

[9] For more information on the Malcolm Smith Motorsports Foundation on the Internet, go to http://www.malcolmsmithadventures.net.

[10] For more information on Wally Dallenbach's Colorado 500 on the Internet, go to http:www.colorado500.org.

[11] For more information on the Blue Ribbon Coalition on the Internet, go to http://www.sharetrails.org/.

Dave and his friend Dale Walksler, curator of the Wheels Through Time Museum, on whose board Dave serves.

Hall of Fame, Dave supports the organization through personal contributions, in-kind support, service on its Board of Directors, and by sometimes loaning motorcycles and artifacts from his personal collection for exhibits at the museum. Peter Gagan, President of the Antique Motorcycle Club of America and also a member of the Motorcycle Hall of Fame Board of Directors, says, "Dave is a wealthy guy, but you would not know it. He does not put on airs or flaunt his money. He has no personal agenda, but is involved only because he wants to help." In addition to financial support from the Dave and Barbara Mungenast Foundation, each year Classic Motorcycles LLC includes a fund raising solicitation for the Motorcycle Hall of Fame Museum in its annual calendar mailing.[12]

The Wheels Through Time Museum was created in 1986 by former Harley-Davidson motorcycle dealer Dale Walksler in Mt. Vernon, Illinois. Walksler first met Dave Mungenast in the mid-1990s. He explains, "We had outgrown every banking relationship in our community, and I began to solicit St. Louis bankers.

[12] For more information on the Motorcycle Hall of Fame Museum on the Internet, go to http:www.motorcyclemuseum.org. For more information on Classic Motorcycles LLC on the Internet, go to http://www.classicmotorcyclesllc.com/.

Barbara and Dave at the St. Louis Boys' Club.

One bank sent a vice president to see our operation, and Dave came along with him. I believe Dave was on the board of the bank at the time, and he was clearly qualified to evaluate a motorcycle dealership. I showed Dave my collection and put him on a 1948 Harley with sidecar, and he hauled the bank officer around awhile. We have been fast friends ever since." Walksler sold his Harley-Davidson franchise in 2000 and moved his collection of over 100 antique motorcycles to a new purpose-built facility in scenic Maggie Valley, North Carolina. Upon creating a new corporation to run the new Wheels Through Time Museum, he asked Dave Mungenast if he would serve on its board. Walksler says, "Dave not only agreed to serve on my board, but he sent his own staff from Classic Motorcycles to help me move my collection from Illinois to North Carolina." He adds, "Dave's philosophy of life is based on service to others. Dave has a lot because he gives a lot. Because he believes that's how it works, he is a fountain of support for others." Walksler concludes, "Dave brings people up. He will always choose the higher road, and he makes serving people feel good."[13]

While Mungenast certainly saw charity modeled within his family of origin, long-time friend and Honda Riders' Club Manager Charlie Keller believes that these practices were reinforced

[13] For more information on the Wheels Through Time Museum on the Internet, go to http://www.wheelsthroughtime.com/.

Barbara and Dave are honored by Marygrove for their charitable support in 2004.

by Dave's study of Soichiro Honda and his attitudes about the relationship between business and community. Keller states, "Dave is a giver. He gives back to the community in which he lives. This is a key part of the Honda philosophy. Mr. Honda preached that one should return wealth and service to the community from which he has achieved his success." Keller adds, "Of course, a person who has a great deal can easily give monetarily. Dave also gives what you cannot get back, and that is time."

In the early days of his international motorcycling career, Dave Mungenast met and formed a lifelong friendship with John

Penton, American national off-road endurance champion and father of the Penton motorcycle. Penton is Mungenast's elder by almost a decade, and by most measures would be viewed as his mentor in the relationship, twice placing Dave on his International Six Day teams. However, the relationship is not quite that simple, because in some respects John regards himself the pupil rather than the mentor. When asked what it is he has learned from Dave Mungenast, John Penton responds, "Dave taught me how to give back. He taught me the importance of giving back to the community that has been so good to me."

CHAPTER ELEVEN

Dave Mungenast: Taking It to the Limit

The year 1975 was an uncertain time in the Mungenast household. Motorcycle sales had become erratic, it was not yet known that Honda cars would become a market leader, Toyota sales were improving but Dave was at odds with the company and its regional manager, and Volvos were at their nadir for quality. Speaking about the automobile business as a whole, Volvo importer and Dave's friend Bob Sinclair recalls, "It was a bad time for dealers, and especially those who were interested in customer satisfaction. No one was satisfied, and a lot of dealers were just doing whatever they could to push iron off the showroom floor." In addition, Dave's international motorcycling career was coming to an end, and in the Fall of 1975 he would compete in his last ISDT on the Isle of Man, failing to finish due to an injury. It was also the year that the Eagles released "Take it to the Limit."

You know I've always been a dreamer.
But the dreams I've seen lately keep on turning out
and burning out
and turning out the same . . .

So put me on a highway and show me a sign,
and take it to the limit one more time.

Dave Mungenast, veteran of nine ISDTs.

It would become Dave Mungenast's favorite song, and its title would seem to be the mantra by which he would patiently and systematically build his businesses, seeking new highways of opportunity, taking one risk after another, and going to the limit time and again to achieve success upon success. Over the next decade he would embark on a risky and exciting career as a motion picture stuntman while becoming the largest Honda car dealer in his market, then be chosen as one of the first Acura dealers in America.

Often, we associate this kind of success with flamboyance, aggressive tactics, and self-absorption, if not during the formative years then at least after success is achieved. With Dave Mungenast, it has not been this way at all. Dave says, "I know dealers who struggled and sacrificed to make it, just like I did. Then one day you see them at a dealer convention and they are wearing big rings and gold chains, they have a new trophy wife, and the wife who sat in the back office and suffered over the numbers and fielded calls from creditors while the company was trying to make ends meet is no longer around." He adds, "That's not the kind of dealer I wanted to be." This observation illustrates several aspects of Dave Mungenast's character. It reveals the quality of personal modesty that has not changed with success, and it illustrates his concern about reputation, not just his own but that of automobile dealers as a whole. Throughout his career he has taken it as a personal challenge to upgrade the quality and image of the business, and this desire carried him to the chairmanship of the St. Louis Automobile Dealers Association, then eventually to the chairmanship of the American International Automobile Dealers Association, where he frankly advised his fellow dealers that they should be running the kind of business where they would be proud for their own children to work. Atlanta Honda and Acura dealer Keith Campbell—also a vintage motorcycle collector and enthusiast—says, "Dave is genuinely concerned about the reputation of the car business." In regard to his personal reputation, Don Levin declares, "One of the most important things to Dave is his name and reputation." Tina Yeager concurs, "To be a successful businessman with a good reputation is what's important to Dave." His administrative assistant Patty Ramsey agrees, "Reputation is everything to Dave. I am proud to say I work for him because he has such a good reputation in town."

Big rings and gold chains are not for Dave, and in regard to his modest personal style, more than one of Dave's friends has affectionately likened him to an old shoe. St. Anthony's Hospital CEO Tom Rockers says, "You can tell a lot about a man by his office. Dave's office is like a comfortable den in someone's home. Its walls and surfaces are covered with photos and memorabilia,

Dave in costume on the set of "Hooper," where he was jerked out of the saddle of a speeding motorcycle after giving Burt Reynolds a ticket.

but they have not been chosen to impress a visitor. They all relate to happy times in Dave's life, and they are there for his own satisfaction." In fact, Dave's office is not even designed for business meetings. It is tucked away on the second floor of his preowned Honda dealership, accessible through an almost hidden stairway and another small office used by Patty Ramsey and Sandy Silvey. Dave is more likely to have business meetings in one of the dealership conference rooms, or at a restaurant, reserving his office for comfortable conversations with friends and key members of his staff.

With new Lexuses and Acuras at his disposal, Dave arrives at his office each morning, typically driving a pickup, wearing jeans,

Vintage bike, vintage event, vintage rider: Dave brings out his 1973 Triumph to ride the 30th anniversary of the American Six Days in 2003.

an open-neck shirt, and sneakers. Even for important business meetings, he will wear a comfortable blazer. Expensive and tailored suits are just not his style, and whether dressed up or dressed down, he wears no jewelry. When they got married, Dave and Barbara got matching wedding bands, but Dave never got in the habit of wearing his since, at that time, he was still a working mechanic, and any mechanic smart enough to value his fingers does not wear rings. Dave wears a Rolex watch, but it is a stainless steel model that he bought second-hand from Don Levin 35 years ago! Revealing a little sheepish guilt, Dave says,

Visiting an old friend: Dave mounts his 1973 Triumph Six Days bike, on display at the Motorcycle Hall of Fame Museum in 2000.

"On the 25th anniversary of our business, Dave, Jr. presented Barbara and me with matching gold Rolexes. She sometimes wears hers, but mine is still home in the drawer. I just hope David understands how much I appreciate the gift."

Certainly, all three of the sons understand their father's motives and his personal style. He never uses clothes, cars, trappings, or other signals of personal wealth to intimidate others or create an appearance of authority. Nor does he practice the rituals of American business. For example, he never learned how to play golf, and never thought it necessary to do so. Both Dave's

Dave does his famous Rokon starting act at a Six Days Reunion.

longtime motorcycling friend Dave Charleville and his accountant Steve Henson credit some of this modesty and absence of pretense to his community and family of origin. Charleville says, "It is part of the south side St. Louis ethic. They were artisans and skilled workers; modest and humble. If they had money, money was not what was important to them. Dave did not run with people with money and behaving like he has it never became important to him." Henson remarks similarly, "While Dave can be a huge risk-taker in business, in terms of personal style he is extremely conservative, and this is characteristic of the culture he grew up in. People in North County dress and drive around in cars that show they have money. A lot of people in South County have money; they just choose not to show it." Mel Elliott, Vice President of the Greater St. Louis YMCA, says, "You would never know he has a lot of money. He does not flaunt his wealth." Bob Sinclair remarks, "He is personally frugal. He will never buy the latest thing when what he has will suffice." Dave's friend Tom Heininger relates a story about his frugality. Tom says, "We were in Daytona with a big group of famous ex-racers, and Dave

With fellow Motorcycle Hall of Famers John Penton and Lars Larsson.

was taking pictures. We were all going to be at a Hall of Fame breakfast the next morning, and I suggested to Dave that he get the shots developed and bring some prints to distribute to everyone." Tom continues, "Dave looked a little troubled and said, 'I don't know. I have about a half roll of film left,' and everyone gave him a hard time about being so cheap." Tom concludes, "The next morning Dave showed up and he had the prints. I said, 'Oh, a big spender after all. You wasted a whole half roll of film, just for us!' and Dave replied, 'It's okay, I explained my situation to the girl where I got the pictures developed, and she gave me a free replacement roll of film.'"

When he takes a business meeting, Mungenast would rather go to a restaurant he considers comfortable than one that is fancy, expensive, or fashionable to be seen in. His old friend Ron Huch laughs about the time when Dave was visiting American Honda in California, and had been assigned a company car and driver.

Six Days veterans Dick Mann, John Penton, and Dave at the 30th anniversary of the American Six Days in 2003.

Huch says, "When his driver asked him where he would like to be taken for dinner, Dave wondered if they could just make a pass through the drive-thru at the In-and-Out Burger." Huch laughs, "Dave loves In-and-Out Burgers, and they don't have them in St. Louis." Don Levin, who has been with Dave for nearly 40 years, concurs, "He can be as plain as an old shoe. He would as soon get a taco as a two-hour dinner." Mungenast's modest personal style is reflected also in his behavior. Don Emde, who has served with him on the board of the Motorcycle Hall of Fame, says, "Dave never talks about himself, neither about what he's done or what he's planning to do." Six Days rider John Greenrose concurs, "He is unpretentious. Even though he has a string of car dealerships and nineteen other things going on, you would never know it. He never boasts about anything." Dave's younger brother Carl says, "Dave does not talk about his financial accomplishments because they are not on his list of what is important." Friend and fellow motorcycle collector John Sawazhki recounts, "One time Barb asked me, 'How many Daves do you know?' I thought about it and realized there is the motorcycling Dave, the car dealer Dave, the property develop-

Dave and his old friend Malcolm Smith during a Baja Ride, 2004.

ment Dave, the philanthropist Dave, the community booster Dave, the outdoorsman Dave, and on and on. People who know him well in one aspect of his life may not even know all the other Daves even exist. That's because he never talks about himself, nor does he do all those things for recognition." St. Louis Acura General Manager Ron Ribolzi has stated, "Dave does not boast about anything. He lets the results speak for him." Fellow Six Days team member Malcolm Smith remarks, "He never puts

himself on a pedestal." Bob Sinclair asserts, "Dave's humility is not an artifice. It is real and a cornerstone of his character."

While Mungenast's down-to-earth nature—including his personal modesty and his comfortable dress—is no artifice, he has learned to use it as his best sales and leadership tool. When with other people, whether chatting with employees, listening to a customer, or sitting in a board room, Dave never becomes the center of attention. Dave Larsen says, "His success as a salesman is based on the fact that he has the ability to make people comfortable immediately. He is in the moment and focused 100 percent on what they have to say. He makes them feel like what they say and who they are is important." Then Larsen adds, "With Dave, what you see is what you get. People can sense his integrity and honesty, and it makes them feel safe." American Honda's Charlie Keller observes, "Dave is a person who can communicate with anybody at any level. He is always quick to remember your name, and he makes other people comfortable." Fellow St. Louis motorcycle dealer Cathy Donelson states, "Dave is a real person. He has not gotten a big head. He is down to earth and he can talk to anyone." Swedish Six Days rider Lars Larsson, who first met Dave in Zachopane, Poland almost four decades ago, concurs, stating, "He is the same man I met in 1967." One-time employee Brian Slark says, "Dave does not talk down to employees. He respects your opinion even if he does not agree, in which case he will ask questions to try to better understand." ManCo accounting director Vatia Flach says, "People are not intimidated by him because there is no air of superiority about him." Bob Sinclair remembers a time when Dave introduced him at an AIADA dinner and said, "Bob Sinclair is the man who taught me how to have fun." Bob says, "That's just absurd, that I taught Dave how to have fun! But it speaks to his character. He is always so ready to give someone else credit, and he wants to say something that will make others feel comfortable." Boys' Club Director Tom Wild remarks, "Both Dave and Barbara Mungenast have the talent to make you feel you are the most important person in the room."

The same quality can be seen in group situations. Jeff Smith, a former motocross world champion who served with Dave on the board of the Motorcycle Hall of Fame Museum says, "He can relax a room." Bob Sinclair, who also served on the same board with Smith and Mungenast, adds, "In board meeting he listens, analyzes, then generally makes a comment that is right on. Oth-

Dave is inducted into the Motorcycle Hall of Fame in 2000.

erwise, he does not say much. When he talks, people listen, and he brings a leveling and tempering influence to the board meeting." Mungenast often uses humor to make people comfortable, but he never tells ethnic or sexist jokes, or jokes at the expense of someone else. Often, his humor is self-effacing. Bob Sinclair relates that once at a charity celebrity riding event, Dave noted his and Bob's 20-year-old riding gear and said, "Look at us, Bob. We look like two living fugitives from a motorcycle museum." About the luncheon where he was invited to become involved in the Boys' Club of St. Louis, Dave later told Tom Wild, "That was the most expensive free lunch I ever had."

Despite his humility and down-to-earth nature, Mungenast is capable of communicating with members of either party at the highest and most powerful levels of government, which has proven a valuable asset for his business, the St. Louis Automobile Dealers Association, and the American International Automobile Dealers Association. He has met with several American presidents, including Ronald Reagan, George W.H. Bush and Bill Clinton, and important legislators, such as Bob Dole and Richard Gephardt. Kurt Mungenast explains, "In political situa-

tions, Dad is skilled at focusing on the issues and now allowing himself to be drawn into partisanship. Just as he is capable of working with all kinds of people, he is good at dealing with government leaders of any persuasion and at every level."

Along with a good sense of humor, Mungenast brings a calm and even temperament to any situation. Patty Ramsey, who works closely with Dave on a daily basis, says, "You will never see Dave get angry. Dave can get angry. People who lie to him or fail to perform without reason make him angry, but you would never know it. Dave does not get mad, he gets quiet." She adds, "In over 15 years, I have never heard him raise his voice." Banker John Tacke says, "In my business, you see a lot of angry people, and for the many years I worked with Dave, I never saw him get angry." Dave Crafton, who works daily in the competitive and high-stress world of automobile dealers, marvels at Mungenast's temperament, stating, "I seldom come across men that are this laid-back. How can someone who is dealing with so many things never get angry? I have never heard him raise his voice." Body shops manager Wayne Lee recounts, "I've never seen Dave mad. I've seen him with a worried look on his face, but he is always in control."

There is one community that enjoys a side of Dave that is not seen by most of his colleagues in the automobile business and the St. Louis business community. Motorcycling has a special place in Mungenast's heart, and among motorcyclists he is a slightly different and special person. Dave has loud, garish, custom-made shirts that he wears only to motorcycle functions. They are in the Hawaiian style, but rather than palm trees or flowers, they are covered with multicolored images of motorcycles. Just to speak of them makes Barbara Mungenast roll her eyes in mock embarrassment. Barbara says, "Dave is very modest and low-profile, but there is a side of him that really likes attention," and clearly the attention he likes best is among his motorcycling buddies. When Dave arrives at a motorcycle event in one of his special shirts, there is a smile on his face and a twinkle in his eye. He delights in seeing other people's reaction, and he throws a knowing grin to those who respond with shock and awe. On these occasions he is especially jovial and light-hearted and quick with a joke. Jeff Heininger says, "Dave has shy and outgoing sides to his personality, and he plays them both." Sometimes, at off-road events, Dave will perform his ritual of the Rokon. Whereas everyone present knows of his wealth, Dave will arrive

Dave and motocross world champion Torsten Hallman at the Motorcycle Hall of Fame Museum in 2005.

in a pickup truck with his 30-year-old Rokon in the back. This is an unorthodox motorcycle with a snowmobile-type variable-speed drive and a lawnmower-type rope pull starter that many considered a joke the day it was built. Wearing his 20-year-old riding gear, Dave will use an old plank—not a nice aluminum ramp—to unload the bike from the back of his truck. Like some kind of medicine show huckster, he will announce to his audience, "No clutch to slip, no gears to strip!," then with a great flourish pull the rope starter to bring the motorcycle to life with sound and fury and a cloud of acrid smoke, eliciting great cheers and jeers from the crowd. Of course, it is even funnier when the Rokon won't start. Jack Penton, a fellow Six Days rider and the son of the legendary John Penton, says, "There is no doubt about it. We motorcyclists get the best of Dave."

Dave Mungenast's personal qualities are reflected in his approach to business, where he is noted for his integrity, systematic approach, determination, loyalty, positive attitude, ability to focus, and large vision. Brian Slark, who helped Dave launch Classic Motorcycles when it was planned to be a restoration business, reports, "Dave modeled positive thinking. He taught me about the power of optimism. He is a great motivator because of his positive attitude because it rubs off on everyone who is in contact with him." Don Emde, owner of a motorcycle industry communications company, concurs, stating, "With Dave there is nothing not to like. I've never had an experience when he was not happy and positive. Never had anything other than a pleasant conversation with him." Fellow off-road motorcyclist John Greenrose sees in Dave's determination an approach similar to the way one approaches a grueling endurance event, such as the Six Days. He says, "Dave will run it through to the end, not quitting until he is finished. No matter how difficult it gets, he will keep going." Carl Mungenast agrees: "Dave is persistent. Persistence is the bellwether of everything he has done. He finds something he believes in, and you can't stop him." Charlie Keller states, "Dave is very methodical, systems oriented, and fiercely loyal to the people who try hard and do their best to do well." Kurt Mungenast concurs: "Many times, Dad will take loyalty over performance." Fellow motorcycle dealer Carl Donelson says, "He has high integrity. He is trustworthy and his word is good. He made it through hard times because bankers and everyone else learned they could trust him." Dave's first lender, bank manager John Tacke, relates, "Over a lifetime of banking, you may meet five or ten people that you can totally rely on. Dave would never walk away from a debt or an obligation." Malcolm Smith adds, "I think Dave has never cheated or been unfair to anyone." Mel Elliott states, "Dave has tremendous integrity. His customers know that and that is why they go to him. And it is why they will send their friends to him." Former employee Pat O'Mara says, "Dave believes that when you say you are going to do something, you do it, and you do it right the first time." Motorsports physician Richard Meyer states, "Dave's best quality is his ability to focus. Whatever he is doing, he is doing 110 percent." Lars Larssen says, "He is an example of what you can do when you have vision." Vatia Flach agrees, "Dave has a very big vision, and he has passed it on to his sons."

There is little doubt that Dave Mungenast learned many of his core values in his family of origin, yet he has expressed them differently from his father. Andy Mungenast was a devout Catholic who went to mass every day. Dave has not abandoned his religion, but his practice is not so overt. Mel Elliott says, "He has strong Christian values, and he walks the talk." Yet, talking the talk is not what Dave does. His faith is far more private. Tom

Rockers, a fellow Catholic and CEO of St. Anthony's Medical Center, says, "Dave has faith, but it is not expressed like his dad's faith was." Keith Campbell says, "Most of my business discussions are with Dave, Jr. Senior and I talk more about raising kids and family than about business. I know that he practices and believes in the power of prayer, but his religion is personal." Dave's brother Carl states, "He is a wise man and a good human being. He has a strong sense of what is right and wrong. He is not an organized religion kind of guy, but he has a very strong faith in something larger than we are." Speaking of the values embodied in members of the family, Dave's sister-in-law Virginia Mungenast says, "Dave is not who he is because he was raised by strict Catholics. It is because he was raised by good people." However, perhaps because of his Christian upbringing, Mungenast embraces a concept of grace that is the foundation of his humility. About his remarkable success in business, he says, "I am very lucky. Getting into the motorcycle and car business with no money. Getting Toyota before anyone could pronounce it. Having Edison Dye call me about the Six Days when I didn't even know what it was. Getting into the movies. Barb says, 'You're in the flow. You are very lucky.'" Clearly, Dave Mungenast sees himself not as a self-made man, but as a blessed man, which is the kind of thinking that was modeled by his father. He also believes in retribution. Discussing business practices, he says, "You'll get paid back for the bad stuff."

One reason Dave has succeeded is because he has never stopped learning. The young man who despised school has become the adult who never leaves the classroom. He has studied the ideas of all of the leading business experts, but, more importantly, he views his day-to-day living as part of an endless learning process. He has experienced business setbacks, and he has found partnerships especially problematic. About these occasions, Dave says philosophically, "When I make a mistake or have a business setback, I try to look at it as just another class in school. Then I remind myself, 'What you don't want to do is repeat the course.'" The goal of endless learning is continuous improvement, what the Japanese call "Kaizen." Ray Mungenast says, "Dad has studied the Japanese culture, and he believes in a philosophy of never-ending improvement, not just in the company, but for the self." Kurt Mungenast affirms this: "Continuous improvement is important to Dad. He takes care of his body and mind, and is always learning." Dave, Jr. concurs, "With Dad,

'constant' is the operative word. He is never idle. We go to the farm, and even when he is not busy, he is picking up rocks." Pat O'Mara declares, "Dave is a very good student about anything and everything he does."

With his financial future secure and his automobile and motorsport enterprises in the capable hands of his sons and veteran employees, one might question why he continues to come to work every day and to constantly seek out new business opportunities which amount to new ways to risk his resources. No one would think the less of him if he withdrew to tend his land and devote his time to the horses, bison, llamas, and longhorn cattle at his ranch. Very simply, Dave Mungenast is not wired that way, and anyone who knows him well will confirm that his motivation is not, nor has it ever been, making money. Rather, he is motivated by the risk, the deal, and the belief he can still make something better for his community and his descendants. Carl tells a story about playing Monopoly when they were young. He says, "Most of the other kids were trying to hoard piles of cash. Dave would be over there with no money at all, spending every penny he could scrape up on another piece of property. He figured out quickly that winning the game was not about getting and accumulating money." Accountant Steve Henson, who understands Mungenast's business philosophy better than anyone else, says, "Dave is not motivated by money. For him, money is not an end, but a tool." He continues, "Dave gets a kick out of the game. He likes risk. He takes risks with his body, and he likes to take financial risks because he knows that greater risks bring bigger rewards." Malcolm Smith agrees, "Dave is motivated by risk as much as anyone I know." Ron Ribolzi says, "I don't think the money matters to Dave. He likes the win." But Ribolzi adds that Mungenast is not reckless with risk. He explains, "Dave thinks things over a long time before he makes a decision." Dale Walksler confirms this opinion: "Dave takes risks with a large dose of caution." Tina Yeager would agree: "He is a very logical person. He may come back to an issue three or four times with questions before he will make a decision." Steve Henson has described Dave's ability to analyze a business deal for unapparent opportunities as uncanny, so perhaps the risks Dave takes are not as large as they appear to those who lack this talent.

Others point out that Dave Mungenast is motivated by what he enjoys, which includes serving and working with people. Tim Bonagurio says, "It's the people. This is his life. This is what he does. Does he have to do it? No, but this is what he started with and what got him where he is. He likes the hunt, he likes the game, he likes the people. Why would anyone retire who so thoroughly enjoys his job?" American Honda's Charlie Keller echoes this sympathy: "Dave is a people person and enjoys being with people. To him, business is a way to contribute to his community and the people in it. It is his mission, and you can't just put a lifelong mission behind you." Tom Heininger sees the people factor along with the risk-taking curiosity. He says, "Dave is always interested with what is on the other side of the hill, and he is not one to sit still. He desires to provide for those around him, which includes his family and employees." Dave Mungenast, Jr. would agree, "He loves the excitement of putting the deal together. He enjoys people and being with them. He feeds off the excitement of working with others to make something happen." Keith Campbell believes that over time Mungenast's motivation has evolved. He says, "When Dave got started, he was motivated by doing what made him happy. Today, he is at the stage in his life where he is setting the table for his kids and grandkids." Dave's business mentor Bob Schultz has a similar opinion: "Dave wants his businesses to survive and prosper because he wants to provide for his employees and his family."

One of Dave Mungenast's favorite axioms is "Everything in moderation." He says it often, and always with a smile on his face. But how does one reconcile this from a man who likes to take it to the limit every chance he gets? How do you square it with a guy who will risk millions when he doesn't have to, who will soldier on at the Six Days with a broken foot in a borrowed boot because it is too swollen to fit in his own, who will ride a speeding motorcycle off a pier or let a brute like Terry Bradshaw repeatedly toss him against a wall? Longtime friend Jimmy Pfleuger tells a tale from the Colorado 500 that seems anything but moderate. He says, "One of Dave's sons—I think it was David, Jr.—flew by us like we were standing still. Dave started after him, but fell, throwing his shoulder out of place. I helped him pick up his bike and he was laughing. He said, 'Quick, help me get my shoulder back in. I'm sure I can catch him!'" What about this kind of behavior speaks to moderation? Perhaps it is all relative. Moderation for a Six Days rider or a movie stuntman may be different from what you or I would see as moderation. Or, perhaps Dave always says it with a smile because there is an aspect of absurd humor behind it. While it is a wise sentiment, per-

In his 70s, Dave Mungenast still taking it to the limit. His friend Malcolm Smith says, "He still rides like a good 50-year-old!"

haps he realizes that his exciting life is anything but a life of moderation. This apparent contradiction would suggest that Dave Mungenast is a complicated man, and there are many who would agree with that assessment.

Two who know him well—Carl Mungenast and Tom Rockers—would disagree. Rockers says, "Don't confuse everything that Dave is involved in with who he is. His life looks very complex, but Dave himself is not complex. He is really a very straightforward guy who understands why he is on this Earth and what he needs to do." Carl Mungenast has a similar view: "Dave is a man who has learned to be comfortable in his own skin. He is self-confident and likes what he does. Over time, he has identified the few things that make him feel good about himself, and he remains faithful to those things. My brother has learned how to be a happy man."

Still you're coming back, you're running back,
You're coming back for more.

So put me on the highway
And show me a sign,
And take it to the limit one more time.

Take it to the limit,
Take it to the limit,
Take it to the limit one more time.

CHAPTER TWELVE

The Dave Mungenast Way: Success through Service and Constant Improvement

Dave Mungenast's philosophy of moral and ethical business has evolved from two sources: the sense of civic service learned from his father, and Kaizen, the Japanese philosophy of continuous improvement. These influences may come from opposite sides of the planet, but they are really not so far apart.

When Bob Schultz got his first batch of Honda motorcycles in the late 1950s, they all suffered engine failures, not because they were poorly designed or built, but because their carburetors had not been properly set for American gasoline. It fell to Dave Mungenast to repair these machines, and when he began to dismantle their engines, he found something that was light-years beyond the design and quality standards of the British and American motorcycles he was accustomed to working on. He gained a high regard for the new generation of post-war Japanese vehicles, and when he went into business for himself, he began to learn about the design philosophy, the production methods, and the corporate systems from which these vehicles came. He was especially intrigued by Honda's products, which were inseparably linked with the reputation and lore surrounding their namesake, Soichiro Honda. When Honda began his manufacturing operation in 1937, his first product was piston rings. Their metallurgy and quality was so bad, no one wanted them. But Honda went from that miserable beginning to become one of the world's leading engine builders and manufacturer of motorcycles and automobiles because he practiced Kaizen. It is a way of thinking through which Dave Mungenast would fashion his own business.

The Japanese word "Kaizen" means "improvement," and it was adopted as the name for an innovative management philosophy. Kaizen means improvement without spending much money, involving everyone throughout the organization, relying heavily on common sense. It emphasizes evolution rather than radical change, encouraging small and incremental improvements, continuously, day by day. Kaizen is ongoing and never ending, focusing on process rather than results. It emphasizes improving profit by eliminating "Muda," the Japanese word for waste, rather than raising prices. Kaizen is sensitive to the needs of workers, because improvement in comfort, health, attitude, and well being results in the reduction of errors and waste. Kaizen encourages that decisions be made by groups composed of people from many different areas of the company, not by just a boss. Any company that has survived into the 21st century has very likely adopted key principles of Kaizen, whether they realized it or not. Kaizen has brought such standard practices as quality circles and just-in-time inventory. In many companies, Kaizen spawned Total Quality Management, which is the application of rigorous statistical analysis to the measurement of ongoing quality improvement. TQM is much easier to apply to the creation of widgets than the measurement of intangibles, such as the attitude and satisfaction of customers, but many of its statistical analysis techniques have been fed back into systematizing the broader management philosophy of Kaizen. Yet Kaizen goes far beyond manufacturing methodology and business philosophy. It goes beyond the nine-to-five of the job to permeate one's daylong behavior, and indeed it integrates one's job with other aspects of his or her life. It becomes a philosophy of life that drives toward improved relationships, inner peace, and personal satisfaction. When we reflect on the words of Carl Mungenast, who asserts that his brother has become a man who is happy in his own skin, we might conclude Dave arrived there through the practice of Kaizen . . . Kaizen and the satisfaction inherent in serving others, as modeled by Andy Mungenast, his father.

Dave Mungenast has created some simple learning devices through which the philosophy of continuous improvement can be reinforced throughout his organization. One is The Platinum Rule, a subtle but insightful improvement upon the Golden

Rule. The Golden Rule states that we should treat others the way we want to be treated. It promotes courtesy, kindness, and consideration. This is well and good, but why should we presume that others want to be treated the way *WE* want to be treated? The Platinum Rule goes a step farther and tell us to treat others the way *THEY* want to be treated. Of course, practicing The Platinum Rule requires one to pay a great deal of attention to the verbal and non-verbal messages of others. We must first ascertain what it is *THEY* want, which is not always easy. It requires listening, respect, focus, concentration, and tactful inquiry. How The Platinum Rule would apply to selling cars, boats, or motorcycles is obvious. How often have we seen a salesman begin to pitch the model that *HE* understands and likes, or the car on which his commission will be greater, rather than make a thoughtful and diligent effort to learn what the customer wants? But, The Platinum Rule goes far beyond salesmanship, and is essential to the continuous improvement of the product or service you are selling. Carl Mungenast explains, "If you adhere to this idea and strive to give customers what *THEY* want, you begin to realize that engineers and designers and production managers do not define quality. The customer defines quality."

Adherence to The Platinum Rule is what drives the Mungenast dealerships to extraordinary lengths to fix problems and satisfy customers, a practice that is consistent with Kaizen. Honda has created for its dealers a data-based quality evaluation system called Excell, which means EXceeding Customer Expectation Levels for Life. The Mungenast Honda dealership uses the program and has integrated it with ManCo's internally-developed methods of data collection and statistical analysis. Dan Lartonoix, who monitors the program, says, "It is aimed entirely at finding and correcting problems. We find it, fix it, confirm it, and prevent it." Acura, Toyota, and Lexus have similar systems that are used at the Mungenast dealerships in concert with the internal customer satisfaction research operation supervised by Tina Yeager at ManCo. Tom Huber, service and parts director of St. Louis Lexus, says, "We see a complaint as an opportunity to better ourselves. If you try to give the customer what they want, even in a bad situation, they will always come back." Tim Jordan, St. Louis Honda's sales manager, believes you don't avoid problems or satisfy the customer as a last resort. He says, "You fix problems immediately because it costs a lot more in time and money to fix an old problem. And you fix it quick because if one person is saying bad things about you, it cancels out a dozen people saying good things." Wayne Lee, manager of the body shops, asserts, "A happy customer will bring you another dozen customers. Maybe an unhappy one will drive that many away." Dave Mungenast, Jr., ever the practical-minded manager, points out that there is a front side and a back side to customer satisfaction. The front side, of course, is sales. About the back side he says, "You can spend some money now to make a customer happy, or you can spend more money later to pay your lawyer to fight with your customers. By that time you have lost, no matter who wins." Ron Ribolzi, general manager of St. Louis Acura, reports, "We make sure we never abandon a customer. We always take care of them. It is the cornerstone in Dave's philosophy of how to do business." Alton Toyota/Dodge Manager Mark Lemons says, "The Mungenast approach is 180 degrees from most dealerships. I have worked at others, and I've never seen a place that works so hard to put the customer first." Reflecting both the pride and the philosophy of the organization, Tina Yeager says, "We never stay still. We are really good at what we do, but we're going to get better."

Another learning device used in the Mungenast organization is the Four Ps. The Four Ps are People, Product, Philosophy, and Profit. Interestingly, it says something about Dave Mungenast that the Four Ps used to be Three Ps, which included People, Product, and Philosophy. Profit was added to the list more as an afterthought, yet it belongs there because it is necessary for a company to thrive.

People—the customers—are to be treated with courtesy and respect. The Mungenast dealerships pay a lot of attention to first impressions, and systems are set up whereby sales people can get their fair share of opportunities without rushing out to be the first to pounce on a customer. It is also emphasized that customers are both "internal" and "external." External customers are the buying public. Internal customers are one's fellow employees, and they are expected to treat each other with as much respect as they treat a person to whom they hope to sell a car. Treating people the way they want to be treated is emphasized in the service department as well. The Mungenasts are very strong believers in the idea that good service experiences eventually translate into future sales. Regardless of the work done on a car, it is returned to the customer cleaner than when it arrived, and Dave reports that the company is beginning to recruit female service writers. He explains, "More than 50 percent of the people who bring in their cars for service are women, and often they will be more comfortable trying to explain a mechanical problem to another woman." It is a fine point in seeking ways to treat customers as they would like to be treated. Many dealerships treat sales and service departments as if they are distinct profit centers that have no relationship and no reason to communicate with each other. The Mungenast dealerships see them as integral parts of the ongoing customer relationship.

The Mungenasts believe in the *products* they sell, and they conduct extensive training so that sales and service personnel thoroughly understand the product. They also believe they should understand the strengths of their products in comparison to the competition. For this purpose, Don Levin keeps an eye on the competition, carefully studies the new models introduced by competing brands, identifies and analyzes market trends, and regularly conducts seminars throughout the dealerships so that personnel will be aware and up to date on the competitive environment. Typically, dealerships function as revolving doors for car salesmen. They devalue them, pit them against each other, apply enormous pressure to perform, and screw with their commissions until they get fed up and go across the street. Then, when the playing field shifts again, they go somewhere else, and possibly back to the dealership from which they came. These types of salesmen believe that selling is only a matter of technique, and that product is of very little importance. Dave Mungenast would rather hire a young, good salesman who knows nothing about cars—what he calls a "green pea"—than an experienced car salesman with bad habits. He believes it is easier to teach a green pea about the product than to break an experienced car salesman of his bad habits. He says, "Bad salesmen will always gravitate back toward their bad habits, because the bad habits are easier behavior."

The Mungenast *philosophy* teaches that the dealerships and their personnel should strive to be a supportive and contributing member of their community. The dealerships need to be seen as responsible businesses whose interests and concerns carry beyond the boundaries of their parking lots. Thus, there is the emphasis on community service and charitable giving among employees, the programs to support the St. Louis Food Bank and the Polly Klaas Foundation, and the Dave and Barbara Mungenast Foundation, which matches the charitable gifts of employees.

It is appropriate that Dave added *profit* to the Three Ps as an afterthought, because, in a sense, for Dave Mungenast, profit is nothing more than the afterthought of good business. He tells his employees that *profit* is important, but he believes that profit is not the reason for doing business. He believes that profit is a by-product of doing business correctly. The bottom-line goal of the Mungenast dealerships is a two percent annual profit margin. In a business as volatile as motorcycles, boats, and automobiles, this margin provides scant room for error. Yet, when the dealerships make their margin, a portion is given over to charity. Clearly, just accumulating wealth is not central to the Dave Mungenast Way.

Sadly, we live in a time when share value and investor satisfaction has become more important than quality, service, innovation, or corporate reputation. This kind of mentality, where everything is dedicated to ballooning profits and bolstering the bottom line leads to disasters like Enron. It causes blue chip corporations to cook their books. It makes employers reduce benefits and treat people like disposable waste. It results in CEOs earning multi-million dollar bonuses while they are putting armies of people out of work. It encourages megacorps with too much money to gobble up productive businesses for which they have no expertise and no interest, except to plunder their assets. It brings us down and destroys our reputation within the world community. It is the opposite of Kaizen, it is capitalism gone bad, and it is not the Dave Mungenast way. Dave Mungenast still adheres to the old-fashioned view that we should build a product, sell a product, or provide a service primarily to benefit the community in which we live. He believes that it is the mission of a business to provide for the wellbeing of the people it employs and to make its sphere of operation a better place. He believes we work to become better, not to become richer. And, he believes that if we perform these functions well, profit will be the natural and inevitable result. Dave Mungenast says, "Profit is the by-product of business. People, product, and philosophy must come first." Mark Lemons agrees, "If you do your business right, the profits will come."

Dave Mungenast and his sons frequently use the word "family" when they talk about how they operate. Their employees are talked about as their "business family," which is more than just a nice sounding buzzword. It reflects a genuine frame of mind that values people, leads to their good treatment, and results in extraordinary loyalty. Thinking of your employees as an extended family means you cannot treat them like they don't count. St. Anthony's Medical Center CEO Tom Rockers says, "Every CEO I've met who is successful always recognizes that the employees do the work. Dave believes this about his own companies, and he has constantly reinforced it on our board of directors." About the Mungenasts, Director of Accounting Vatia Flach, who has worked at other dealerships, says, "This group is top notch. There is a striving to do better on a daily basis. They not only care about their customers, but they truly care about their employees. They are way above other dealerships for employee benefits." Tim Bonagurio, another with extensive experience at another dealership, confirms, "These guys are more generous toward their employees than anyone I have known. They treat you like family."

In addition to good compensation, the Mungenasts have created many ways to express their gratitude and reward good performance. There is a company picnic, an annual night at the ball game, and a festive Christmas party, a huge dinner and dance that includes employees, former employees, business associates, friends of the family, and friends of friends. The Honda, Acura, and Lexus dealerships conduct monthly award luncheons where top performance is celebrated with praise and monetary awards. Dave, Jr. says, "We recognize high achievers in front of 120 of their peers. It is our policy to praise in public, but counsel behind closed doors." The organization has created a scoring system indexed to sales that takes 50 winners and their families on an annual cruise. And when one of the dealerships wins its manufacturer's top award—which each has done now for many years running—the entire staff and their families are treated to a day at the Six Flags amusement park. Alton Toyota/Dodge Finance Manager Don Lindsay says, "They do so much for their employees, and it is noticed. My wife works for a company that does not even acknowledge Christmas." Ron Ribolzi says, "What you learn from the Mungenasts is how to work and play well with others."

The Mungenasts also believe in promoting from within and encouraging personal and professional development. Tom Huber says, "Their policy is to hire from within. The Mungenasts are really in tune with their employees, and when they see a hard worker, they will invest in their development and help them move up the ladder." Vatia Flach reports, "They encourage employees to take courses related to their work. If you get a C or better, the company will reimburse 50 percent of your tuition. In my case, they have never said "no" to any course I wanted to take." Like many things the Mungenasts do, good treatment of employees is consistent with Kaizen. About their investment in employee development, Ray Mungenast says, "You cannot get good customer satisfaction in this business if you do not have good employee satisfaction. It is not only a practical business philosophy, but it is the right thing to do." How the dealerships treat their employees is demonstrated in staff seniority. Dave Larsen, the first man Dave ever hired, is still with the company after 41 years. Carlo Martellaro has served 40 years; Don Levin, 39 years; Ron Ribolzi, 20 years; Tina Yeager, 18 years; Mark Lemons, 17 years; Vatia Flach, 13 years; Don Lindsay, 9 years. Patty Ramsey came in 1973 and left in 1987 to raise a family. She returned in 1990 and now has served the company for 31 years. Tom Huber started at age 16, left, then returned at 22 and has been with the company for 20 years. And, it should be noted that Ray and Dave, Jr., who have been working in the dealerships since their early teens, have 50 years of experience between them. Vatia Flach says that throughout the whole 450 person organization, including even the entry level jobs, the average tenure is probably above five years. Marketing consultant Dan Borgmeyer says, "Once you are in the Mungenast organization, you become part of the fabric."

With five dealerships, a marina, and extensive real estate holdings, one might wonder how Dave Mungenast handles what he has so efficiently, notwithstanding the fact that he is always looking at new business opportunities. Dave Crafton, who, as executive director of the St. Louis Automobile Dealers Association, has inside knowledge of how all of the major dealerships function, says, "Dave is a good delegator. This is the secret to his productivity." Steve Henson agrees, stating, "He is definitely hands-off. He is the best delegator I have ever seen." In addition, Mungenast knows how to identify the right people for the right jobs, then guide them through trust and leadership by example, rather than explicit instruction. Ray Mungenast says, "Dad is an example setter. He teaches more through example than by instructing or directing. I know where he got it. His parents—my grandparents—were the same way." Dave Larsen, the organization's most senior employee, says, "Once you have proven yourself in Dave's mind, you are pretty much given a free hand." Charlie Keller, who has the advantage of seeing the organization from an outside perspective, says, "Dave is very methodical, systems oriented, and fiercely loyal to the people who do well. He lets them do what they do best." Ed Schmidt, a former employee and fellow Six Days rider who set up the first computerized accounting and information processing systems for the Mungenast dealerships in the early 1970s, says, "Dave is a good manager. He trusts the people he has and is always there for them. He does not look over your shoulder. He motivates by example and leaves you alone to do your job, but he is available when you need him." Tina Yeager says, "He builds your confidence in what you think you can do, then he gets out of the way." Wayne Lee, who has had the opportunity to work with Dave and for Dave, says, "Dave tries to hire and put in place the kind of people who do things the way he does them. He is careful about who he puts in key positions. This is another reason they promote from within, because people coming up through the ranks are a known quantity and already understand how the company operates."

The Dave Mungenast Way, influenced by Kaizen, has built businesses that grow from their own methodology, based on a reputation for integrity and good service. Dave's brother Carl says, "Dave Mungenast has become a brand with an outstanding reputation. People will drive long distances to one of his dealerships because of the brand." Professional colleagues of Mungenast, such as John Tacke and Steve Henson, state that they can recommend the Mungenast dealerships to their friends and other clients with confidence that they will be treated well. As a result, the Mungenast dealerships do very little advertising, relying heavily on their reputation for the growth and customer retention, which is twice that of a typical automobile dealership. The people the Mungenast dealerships have sold cars to are their best advertising medium. About the Mungenast Way, Dave, Jr. states, "I think we've proven that it works. But there are still dealers out there who spend fortunes on advertising and promotions to bring in new customers which they treat like they don't care if they ever see them again. I suppose there always will be." About the Mungenast dealerships, Dave, Sr. says, "We're not here to sell anybody just one car."

Looking back over his long career, thinking of the difficult times when just staying in business was a day-to-day struggle, and pondering the growth from the 1980s onward and the development of a powerful organization based on people, philosophy, and product, Dave Mungenast thinks of one client relationship that is especially satisfying. Back when he was young, unproven, broke, and starting out with Japanese cars and motorcycles, there was a prominent man on the board of the bank where Dave did business who drove Fords, thought Japanese cars were a joke, and considered Mungenast a bad business risk. He constantly counseled against getting in too deep with that crazy Dave Mungenast and his silly little Japanese cars. Today, everything has changed, not the least of which are Japanese cars and this man's attitude. To date, he has purchased two Lexuses from Dave Mungenast. Very likely, they will not be the last.

AUTHOR'S EPILOGUE

The Shepherd of the Hills

The stranger seated himself upon the rude steps. Below and far away he saw the low hills, rolling ridge on ridge like the waves of a great sea, until in the blue distance they were so lost in the sky that he could not say which was mountain and which was cloud. His poet heart was stirred at sight of the vast reaches of the forest, all shifting light and shadows; the cool depths of the near-by woods with the sunlight filtering through the leafy arches in streaks and patches of gold on green; and the wide, wide sky with fleets of cloud ships sailing to unseen ports beyond the hills.

This is a passage from "The Shepherd of the Hills,"[1] by Harold Bell Wright, one of American literature's most beloved books, describing the view experienced by its protagonist after a long, tiring journey into a remote region of the Missouri Ozarks, years before the arrival of the railroad and the growth and popularity of towns like Branson. When he was a child, known to his friend and family as "Trapper Dave," Dave Mungenast read books like "Call of the Wild" and "Shepherd of the Hills" and dreamed of being a mountaineer, living rough and adventurously in grand settings like those described by Harold Bell Wright. Today, Dave owns land in Missouri, Colorado, and Wyoming.

[1] Harold Bell Wright. "The Shepherd of the Hills," Grosset & Dunlap, New York. 1907.

One of these holdings is a thousand acres near Branson where Barry Johnson works in his artist's studio and helps Dave tend a herd of prize longhorn cattle, possibly the only breed tough enough to thrive on the wiry grass of these rocky hills. In a sense, though he has remained deeply immersed in his business life centered mostly in St. Louis, holdings like his land in the Ozarks have enabled Dave to taste that childhood fantasy of the life of an American mountaineer.

Wright's story of 19th century life in the Ozarks is a straightforward and beautifully-written morality tale about a man who redeems his shattered life by living simply and turning his attention to the needs of others. It allegorically describes the mountainous trails that he walks as high roads and low roads and speaks of the choices we all have to take the high or low roads in our lives. Through his quiet example, and drawing upon resources of character that he does not realize he has, the Shepherd saves a family and its community, raising it up morally and culturally without destroying its rich and noble Ozark heritage. "The Shepherd of the Hills" became hugely popular, achieving at least the fourth-highest sales of any book in American history. Some claim it ranks second only to The Bible. It launched a new career and a second life for Wright, who went on to write 19 books. Ironically, it helped popularize the Ozarks and create the cartoon-like entertainment center of Branson, which, at the end of the day, can probably credit its style and character more to Al Capp than Harold Bell Wright.

Before the explosion of Branson, Wright founded the town of Garber, Missouri. Today, Dave Mungenast owns the town of Garber, which amounts to ruins of a school and a post office, protected from total destruction from vandalism by a frail armor of thistles and blackberry bushes. In the process of conducting research for this book, Dave took me to meet his beautiful longhorn cattle and to visit the town of Garber. As we stood among the ruins, Dave began to talk of his dream to restore the town, not as a Disneyesque theme park with employees dressed like Little Abner and Daisy Mae, but as an authentic recreation based on its remaining ruins. "Actually," he said, "I want to mothball it more than restore it. I want to clean it up and find someone who can re-roof the buildings just as they would have at the time they were built, and I want it to become a place where an educational non-profit organization can bring young people to show them how people really lived in the Ozarks before our time." Indeed, there is a great deal more to this man than car sales and commercial development. They are just the means by which he has gained the ability to do his greater work. He actually pulled from his breast pocket a little piece of paper which contained a wish list of what he hopes to do and the investment each item is likely to require. The protection of Garber is just one of many big dreams that Dave told me about that I believe would not be appropriate to reveal on these pages. Just suffice to say they all involve providing for and seeking to lift up the generations to come: his grandchildren and their children. None can be even remotely construed as a monument to himself. Like the Shepherd of the Hills, Dave Mungenast has shifted his attention from the struggles of his own life to the welfare of future lives, and through the dissemination of wisdom through quiet example he lifts others up.

My first thought about his list of dreams was that it seemed unrealistically ambitious for a man of 72. Then, as I thought about Dave's dreams, I was reminded of the opening line of his favorite song, "Take it to the Limit" by the Eagles—*You know I've always been a dreamer*—and it occurred to me that it is the inevitable fate of every great dreamer that he will never fulfill all of his dreams. Even if he achieves extraordinary age, the dreamer will always have in his breast pocket a little list of great things yet to be done. Realization of the dream may not be as important as making preparation and laying the foundation for it. Dave has done that. Furthermore, he stands in a tradition of dreamers. He is a single chapter in the history of a family that can trace its fulfillment of dreams back through the seizing of Okinawa, creation of the JayCees, building St. Louis, winning a war against slavery, and erecting Gothic cathedrals in Europe.

In pursuit of his dreams, Dave Mungenast may have refined the Mungenast Way and learned new ways to apply it, but he did not invent it. Like Kaizen, the way of continuous improvement, the Mungenast Way is a process that has been passed down over many generations, and it will continue to change, adapt, and improve beyond the days of David and Barbara Mungenast. What is important is that they have provided the resources to let this happen, and we're not talking about money. With three sons well raised, and with more than a dozen grandchildren so far, there remain abundant resources to continue the Dave Mungenast Way. About their sons, one of the key employees in the Mungenast business family has said, "In the way they treat people and in their concern for the community, they are trying very hard to carry on the legacy."

APPENDIX A

A Mungenast Chronology

1688 Johannes Munggenast is born in Fehrbach, Baden, Germany. He will become the patriarch of the family line from which the St. Louis Mungenasts descend.

1847 Reinhardt Mungenast and his son Bendict immigrate to America, settling in South St. Louis.

1856 Benedict marries Louisa Munch. The union produces two sons: Joseph and Andrew.

1858 Benedict joins the Missouri Infantry, with which he fights for the North during the American Civil War.

1884 Andrew Mungenast, born in 1864, marries Elizabeth Spindler. The marriage produces six children including Andrew G., Dave Mungenast's father.

1894 Joseph and Andrew Mungenast open Model Hardware Company at 3215 Meramec Street in South St. Louis.

1895 November 22, Andrew G. Mungenast is born.

1915 October 15, the Junior Chamber of Commerce is founded at the Mission Inn restaurant in St. Louis by Henry Giessenbier, its first president; and Andrew G. Mungenast, its first secretary.

1924 August 13, Andy Mungenast, jr. is born.

1934 October 1, David Francis Mungenast is born.

1938 June 10, Barbara McAboy (Mungenast) is born.

1950 Dave buys his first motorcycle, a used 1946 Indian Chief, and wrecks it on the way home.

1952 Dave goes to work as a mechanic for Reiss Automotive, then drives a parts truck for Roberts Chevrolet in St. Louis.

1953 April, Dave meets future bride Barbara McAboy at Mary Ann's Ice Cream Parlor.

Dave and his motorcycle friends form a club, the Midwest Enduro Team.

1954 Dave drops out of St. Louis University and enlists in the Army, joins the Special Forces, goes to Korea, and is picked for the 8th Army Honor Guard.

1957 December, Dave musters out of the service.

1958 Dave goes to work for Bob Schultz's motorcycle dealership in January, returns to school in September, resumes dating Barbara.

1959 January 24, Dave Mungenast and Barbara McAboy are married.

1960 April 1, David Mungenast, Jr. is born.

1961 Dave graduates from St. Louis University with a degree in geography and anthropology, goes to work for the U.S. Aeronautical Chart and Information Center while still holding down a job at Bob Schultz's motorcycle store.

July 17, second son Ray Mungenast is born.

1962 The Mungenast family moves to Lake Montowese.

1964 Dave wins the 24 hour motorcycle marathon at River Dale Speedway, giving Honda its first national championship title in America.

Dave Larsen becomes Dave Mungenast's first employee, hired to help set up a new Honda motorcycle dealership.

November, Dave resigns from the Aeronautical Chart and Information Center in preparation for opening his Honda motorcycle dealership.

1965 January 1, Dave opens his Honda motorcycle dealership, then takes on a Triumph motorcycle franchise near the end of the year.

Dave rides the Jack Pine Enduro, breaks his leg.

1966 Dave wins the Riverdale 24 hour national marathon for a second time.

November, Dave opens his Toyota dealership at 5625 Gravois Avenue in South St. Louis.

1967 Dave rides his first International Six Days Trial in Poland, earns a gold medal; he opens Pacific Cycle Playground, a motorcycle riding park on leased property.

1968 October 15, third son Kurt Mungenast is born.

Dave rides on the U.S. Vase Team at the ISDT in San Peligrino, Italy; earns a bronze medal.

1969 Dave dislocates a shoulder at the Jack Pine Enduro, but goes directly to Germany to ride the ISDT where he earns a silver medal. He earns a gold medal at the Berkshire International Trial in Massachusetts.

1970 Dave breaks his ribs at the ISDT in Spain; fails to finish the event.

Dave opens Doe Run Cycle Park, a 1,700 acre riding area for motocross, trials, and the enjoyment of his motorcycle customers. It continues through 1980.

1971 Dave earns a gold medal at the ISDT at the Isle of Man.

Dave takes a Volvo franchise; keeps it until 1977.

1972 Dave teams up with Jeff Heiniger and Gene Cannady to ride the Baja 1000 for Honda.

Dave rides a works Honda at the ISDT in Czechoslovakia; bike breaks and Dave fails to finish.

1973 Dave earns a silver medal at the ISDT in the United States.

1974 Dave takes on a Honda car franchise.

Breaks his hip at an ISDT qualifying event but still makes the team, earning a bronze medal at Camerino, Italy.

1975 Dave rides his last ISDT at the Isle of Man, but fails to finish due to injury.

The Honda motorcycle store moves to Lindbergh Avenue.

1976 Dave starts his career as a motion picture stunt man; will work in several Burt Reynolds films including "Cannonball Run," "Hooper," and "The End."

Dave's father Andrew G. Mungenast dies.

1977 Dave is stunt double for Christopher Lee, whose character is killed in an underwater scene in "Airport 77."

The Volvo franchise is discontinued.

1978 Dave is featured by the "St. Louis Post-Dispatch" as the top Honda automobile dealer in the city.

1979 Dave sells his St. Louis Toyota franchise due to conflict with the regional representative; will later say that it was the biggest mistake of his business career.

1984 Dave does stunt work with motocross champion Kent Howerton in the movie "Stormin' Home."

Dave participates in a movie stunt in New Zealand for "Welcome to Paradise" where several motorcyclists plunge off a pier into the ocean; earns a nomination for "Stunt Man of the Year" award in 1985.

1986 Starts St. Louis Acura, one of the first Acura dealerships in America.

David, Jr. becomes general manager of the Honda dealership.

1987 Dave acquires a Toyota/Dodge dealership in Alton, Illinois; buys property for ranching and recreation at Lake Table Rock and begins to restore an old country home.

Dave becomes Secretary of the Board of Directors of the Boys' Club of St. Louis, a post that he has held to the present.

1988 Dave hires Brian Slark to run Classic Motorcycles, a business to trade in vintage and collectible motorcycles.

Dave is recognized as "Dealer of Distinction" in *Sports Illustrated.*

1989 Dave opens his St. Louis Lexus dealership.

Ray becomes general manager for the Acura dealership.

1991 Dave's mother Charlotte Bokel Mungenast, dies on November 28.

The Midwest edition of *Time Magazine* recognizes Dave as its "Time Quality Dealer."

1993 The Andrew and Charlotte Mungenast Memorial Library is dedicated at Jaycee headquarters in Tulsa, Oklahoma.

1994 Dave recruits his older brother Tom to be director of operations for his growing businesses.

1998 Dave becomes chairman of the American International Automobile Dealers Association.

July, Kurt musters out of the Marines at the rank of captain; returns to Missouri and goes to work at the Honda dealership.

1999 May 16, Dave's older brother Tom dies following heart by-pass surgery.

The Mungenast family of businesses acquires Wayne's Auto Body.

2000 January 1, Classic Motorcycles LLC opens a museum at the renovated 5625 Gravois, Dave's original Toyota dealership.

Dave is inducted into the Motorcycle Hall of Fame.

Lake of the Ozarks Marina is opened.

2002 Dave becomes Chairman of the American International Automobile Dealers Association.

Dave joins the board of the Wheels Through Time Museum, opening in Maggie Valley, North Carolina in June that year.

Dave joins the board of the Motorcycle Hall of Fame Museum.

2004 Dave receives the American International Automobile Dealers Association Lifetime Achievement Award.

Kurt moves from Honda to lead the management team at the Alton Dodge/Toyota dealership.

April 25, Dave and Barbara are feted as Marygrove Honorees of the Year.

Index

M